# MARRIAGE MATTERS

## TYRONE HOLCOMB

CREATION HOUSE
A STRANG COMPANY

MARRIAGE MATTERS by Tyrone Holcomb
Published by Creation House
A Strang Company
600 Rinehart Road
Lake Mary, Florida 32746
www.strangbookgroup.com

Scripture quotations marked THE MESSAGE are from *The Message: The Bible in Contemporary English*, copyright © 1993, 1994, 1995, 1996, 2000, 2001, 2002. Used by permission of NavPress Publishing Group.

Scripture quotations marked NCV are from The Holy Bible, New Century Version. Copyright © 1987, 1988, 1991 by Word Publishing, Dallas, Texas 75039. Used by permission.

Scripture quotations marked NKJV are from the New King James Version of the Bible. Copyright © 1979, 1980, 1982 by Thomas Nelson, Inc., publishers. Used by permission.

Scripture quotations marked KJV are from the King James Version of the Bible.

Scripture quotations marked NIV are from the Holy Bible, New International Version of the Bible. Copyright © 1973, 1978, 1984, International Bible Society. Used by permission.

Cover and interior photos by AWC Photograph, www.awcphotograph.com

Design Director: Bill Johnson
Cover design by Nathan Morgan

Library of Congress Control Number: 2009943067
International Standard Book Number: 978-1-61638-134-9

10 11 12 13 14 — 9 8 7 6 5 4 3 2
Printed in the United States of America

*This book is dedicated to my sister*
*Nicole*
*May 27, 1969—May 29, 2009*
*Thanks for that never ending smile,*
*unbreakable spirit, and enduring love.*
*Our memories of you will forever be cherished.*
*See you later...*

# CONTENTS

# ACKNOWLEDGMENTS

IT IS WITH GREAT pleasure that I honor the following people without whom this book would not be the work that you have before you.

- The Christian House of Prayer Family—Thank you for your friendship and love.
- Friends—Pop Smiley, Karen Harris, and Clive Hickson, you allowed me to read this book to you from the stages of raw to ready. Your time and eagerness to listen is priceless. Thanks!
- Ramona Johnson—Imagine the kind of book we would have if we ever had enough time to edit it. Thank you for your expert eye and Christlike mind.
- My father—Seeing your relentless love toward Jesus is a true inspiration. Many of the concepts in this book are a direct reflection of your teaching. I am fortunate to be your son.
- My children—This project has stolen some of our time. I look forward to doing some catching up. You all bring me great joy.
- My wife—There is a love that I have for you that could never be put into words. However, I'll do my best to put them into action.
- My Lord—It is because of You and for You that I am who I am. Continue to lavish Your love on me. I need it and am forever grateful.

# FOREWORD

IN TODAY'S SOCIETY WHERE there is so much confusion, distortion, fear and failure in every arena of life the question is, "Does marriage matter?" The obvious answer is yes, marriage matters, without a shadow of a doubt. I believe the Lord inspired this book, *Marriage Matters*. I believe the hand of the Lord came upon Minister Tyrone, and as it is written in the Scripture, Psalm 45:1, "My tongue is the pen of a ready writer." The thing I love about *Marriage Matters* is how easy it is to read and understand. Immediately you can make the midterm corrections and apply the biblical principles that will strengthen your stakes or straighten the crooked things that have been hindering your marriage flow.

The marriage is the first and noblest of all human relationships. Minister Tyrone's *Marriage Matters* gives us a greater appreciation for the union of marriage in that it is more than a contract, it is a covenant between man, woman and God. Even if you are not married, this book will work for you because the principles are universal. It is God's Word, will and way He intended for mankind to relate and function in our society. I know you will be better versus worse for *Marriage Matters*.

It's all about Him!

—BISHOP NATE HOLCOMB

# INTRODUCTION

I T IS MY SINCERE desire that all marriages experience God's grace and goodness. When I think about our God I can't help but become overwhelmed with the idea that He created us with the purpose of experiencing His good life. Sometimes this is difficult to fathom.

We know through scriptures God's desire is for us to live the good life. In the beginning of the recreation, God saw that everything He had made was very good. His intent was to have man surrounded by His goodness. God even spoke through His prophet Joshua telling His people how to have good success (Josh. 1:8) and experience the good life.

Why don't many marriages measure up when it comes to meeting this goal (the good life)? The answer is simple! Not many understand how to tap into the good life that God created for marriage. After speaking to many of my Christian brothers and sisters, I discovered that God's good life is often aspired but hardly acquired. In order to find the good life you must be able to define it. This good life bespeaks love, and there is no true living without loving. This book is designed with the purpose of revealing God's way to the good life of love.

The essential step to possessing the good life is loving God. In case you've missed it, I'll say it again. We *must* love God! Once we love God, our desire is to please Him. Too often, we make the mistake of trying to love our spouse without first loving Him and more importantly without the love of God.

In the Bible, 1 Corinthians 13 is considered the "Love Chapter." I can recall reading this chapter many years ago and feeling so unworthy. I felt unworthy as a husband because what I considered love didn't add up to what God considers love. If you are feeling that your love pales in comparison to God's love, don't fret; the intent of 1 Corinthians 13 is not to measure your love but to magnify His. Clearly understanding this enables us to take the love that He has freely given and administer that same love to our partner for life.

Therefore, let's dissect the vastness of God's love and recapture the mandate of every married Believer—to love our spouse, unconditionally.

If this book is successful, you will have an unbreakable bond and a marriage that is marinated in the good life of God. Read it knowing that marriage matters and what matters most is "To love and to cherish."

# one

# ARE WE THERE YET?

*Love Is Patient*
*1 Corinthians 13:4*

**M**ARRIAGE CAN SOMETIMES CREATE the illusion that struggles are easier to overcome with someone to help tackle them. This idea is true. However, what many couples come to discover is there can be more struggles inside the home than the trials that mount up on the outside. To overcome the struggles of marriage takes love manifested through patience.

A marriage free from struggles, stress and strife is highly sought after like a pauper seeks a winning lottery ticket. Frustrations often escalate when couples expect their marriage to be a utopia. Seeking paradise is not to be preferred over settled patience, like children in the backseat of life who ask the question, "Are we there yet?" Don't become impatient waiting on a good marriage.

> A good marriage is not so much finding the right person as being the right person.[1]
> —SCOTT ROWLEY

Goodness can be equated with maturity. For something to be considered good the timing must be right. Many find themselves asking when will their marriage develop to the state of goodness or maturity. The question is not will your marriage ever come to a place of maturity, but rather, will you mature in the place of marriage? When you learn to love through the art of patience, you're on your way. Loving with patience means you allow your spouse the opportunity to grow and become who God intended. Loving with patience means you don't *decide*, you *discover* who your spouse is as a person. Therefore, don't attempt to change your spouse; allow them to develop through the grace of God.

## PATIENCE SEEKS PROGRESS

I wasn't forewarned of the challenges I would encounter as a new husband. I imagined life with a woman who had her priorities and personality in order. My wife can testify that she looked for the same things in a husband. Although both of us had cracks in our own character, I still expected my wife to be Wonder Woman, and she was seeking Superman. It didn't take long for us to figure out that we had received normal human beings with frailties and faults.

This eye-popping revelation is not exclusive for my marriage alone. Many couples marry with high and lofty expectations of hooking up with the perfect mate, but are awakened to the reality that perfection only exists in dreamland. I've had many counseling sessions (more than I care to count) where couples complain about growing weary of their partner's shortcomings. My advice has been and continues to be—don't look for perfection, look for progress.

A man came in fourth place in a race. When he crossed the finish line, he threw his arms up in victory and began to celebrate. This display of victory seemed awkward and out of place because no prizes were given to fourth place finishers. Puzzled, a news reporter asked the runner why he reacted in such an exuberant manner. The runner explained with a smile on his face, last year I came in sixth.

Ma'am, your husband may not help with the house cleaning, but does he appreciate you for cleaning? Mister, your wife may not be as passionate as you are about some things, but does she listen to you express your passion? Patience says, "Until I receive my desired results, I'm satisfied with progress."

If you're going to progress, you must practice. Practice means making an assertive effort to ensure that your marriage works. When your spouse does the wrong thing, you must continue extending love with patience. I hear you saying, "I have been patient, how long should I wait to see change?" The answer is until change comes. Change comes through practicing every day.

> The greatest of all insights is that we cannot be tomorrow what we do not do today.[2]
>
> —JOHN C. MAXWELL

This quote simply means that whatever you hope to receive, you must begin to work on now. If you want a good marriage you must patiently practice goodness in your marriage. When things happen to challenge its sanctity don't give up or give in; continue to progress with patience.

## PATIENT ON PURPOSE

How do you react when your spouse doesn't say or do everything you like? Do you panic or wonder if marriage was the right choice? Should you blame God for not intervening and protecting you from the mess that is associated with marriage? Of course not! You should discover what love is and the power that love possesses.

Love's power is not an accidental discovery. You have to look for it. Simply put, seek reasons to continue in the love that you have for your spouse, regardless the mistakes.

First Peter 4:8 (NKJV) reads:

> And above all things have fervent love for one
> another, for "love will cover a multitude of sins."

The preceding scripture is not suggesting that we make excuses for our spouse's behavior, nor is it promoting a cover-up of their faults. It is conveying that we become patient on purpose.

Therefore, patience must not be used every now and then; it must become a part of your mentality and makeup. Patience is intentional and paramount when demonstrating the God kind of love. You have to aggressively go after it. Hence, it is absolutely critical to comprehend patience.

Consider the account with God's servant Noah. Noah had to exhibit patience while obeying God and building that massive boat. He did not know God's exact plan, nor did he totally understand the predicament he would face because of the flood. Although Noah wasn't sure of his project, he placed his faith in God and step by step worked toward the promise (his deliverance). Think with me. In the process of time, *every day*, Noah had to have patience on purpose. Through the barrage of questions from neighbors, "What are you building?" "What is rain?" without knowing the answers, because he knew his God, Noah worked with faith and patience. In the end, the project was for his protection.

The boat Noah built protected him and his family. He couldn't risk a quick fix and short cuts were out of the question. To short change the project would have spelled certain death. Noah's patience prevailed and eight human lives were spared.

Are you willing to forgo patience for a quick fix? I hope not. Like Noah, God has a project for you to complete. Noah's project was a massive boat; your project is your marriage. Like Noah, the completion of your project will spare you, your spouse, your children, and perhaps countless others from numerous disasters. Don't look for a quick fix. Be patient on purpose!

## Patience Brings Pleasure

When you married, you anticipated enjoying life with your spouse and expected your spouse to provide you pleasure. If that was your thought, it's okay; after all, the old adage, "I can do badly all by myself" has much truth in it. To say that patience brings pleasure is to understand you can't abort the mission. Many have disqualified themselves from God's blessings because they didn't have the stuff that sticks. The stuff is patience. The Scripture admonishes us,

> My brethren, count it all joy when you fall into various trials, knowing that the testing of your faith produces patience. But let patience have its perfect work, that you may be perfect and complete, lacking nothing.
> —James 1:2–4, NKJV

Our patience must go to work. In the natural, when you go to work you receive wages. So it is with this spiritual principle. To receive the full pleasure God has placed in your spouse you must be patient for it. When it comes to pleasing your spouse, don't beat yourself up because you haven't become what your spouse desires. If it is not in violation of God's Will for your life, He will help you develop into the person He created you to be. And, that will no doubt please your spouse.

Let's consider three particular areas where we must exhibit patience concerning our spouse:

1. Their actions
2. Their attitudes
3. Their articulation

**Actions—the fact or process of doing or acting**

If you grew up in America you have heard the sayings, "actions speak louder than words" or "put your money where your mouth is." These sayings and others like them have helped shape the way we think about what others do. If not careful, we can begin to judge our spouse on the merit of their actions alone.

I can recall, in the first year of my marriage I used to hang out with some friends, and at the end of the day I would pick up some fast food to take home for myself. Not the most nutritious meal I know, but what can I say? I'm a part of the fast food generation. Upon returning home, my wife would ask what I brought her to eat. My answer would be, "Nothing!"

Disappointedly she would say, "If you loved me, you would have brought me something home." Then I would become offended by the suggestion that my love was lacking because I would come home empty handed. My reasoning was, she was home all day, and surely she ate something. Nonetheless, Andrea felt that I was being inconsiderate by not at least offering. I'm happy to report; she has me well trained now. I won't come home with candy for myself without calling to see if she would like some. However, my point is that my love for Andrea wasn't lacking. It's just that I thought differently about that particular situation (action). I asked Andrea to count it to my head not to my heart.

Most marriages suffer because people take various acts the wrong way. Your spouse may do some things differently, but don't hold that against them. Discuss your differences and allow patience and love to prevail over any problem, and the differences will begin to diminish. Whatever you do, don't make the mistake of taking every action and defining it as love or the lack thereof.

**Attitudes—a settled opinion or way of thinking**

The beauty and miracle of marriage is that you have two people, with two different upbringings coming together in union with one another. Knowing this, we must understand that there will be occasions when the two won't see eye to eye. Each will have their own attitudes and opinions. If your spouse happens to have a unique way of seeing things don't despise that, learn to appreciate their perspective.

Patience gives grace to the couple and allows them the time and space to eventually develop the same or similar perspectives on life. This occurs naturally and does not have to be forced upon either person. As you go through similar trials and celebrate the same triumphs you'll began to have comparable attitudes.

Andrea and I don't always agree on how to approach certain occurrences, but that's okay. Sometimes her way is the best and when the stars are aligned I can strike gold and come up with a good idea, too. In either case, we agree to have patience with one another and continue allowing growth to take place in each other.

Finally, attitude does not only deal with what a person thinks, it reveals *how* a person thinks.

In an attempt to make an elderly woman's transition into the nursing home a smooth one, the attending nurse decided to escort the elderly woman to her room. As the nurse began to describe the room, the elderly woman enthusiastically shouted, "I love it!" "But you haven't seen the room yet," the nurse responded. "That doesn't have anything to do with it," the elderly woman replied. "Happiness is something you decide on ahead of time. Whether I like my room or not doesn't depend on how the furniture is arranged. It's how I arrange my mind."

When you exhibit the right kind of attitude, you will have patience with your spouse and you'll make it a lot easier for them to have patience with you.

### Articulation—the act of speaking

Unfortunately, I have had to referee couples in counseling sessions because of what was spoken out of context. There have even been complaints about what has *not* been said, namely, "I love you."

Let me explain. Women, in most cases, are well versed at speaking and in particular at expressing how they feel. As a rule of thumb, not only are women *able* to communicate, they are also *willing* to communicate. Men, on the other hand, find it difficult to articulate their emotions. Within recent years these roles have reversed. In either case, the spouse who finds it easy to communicate must be patient with the one who doesn't.

I mentioned how I have refereed sessions where one spouse has expressed disappointment that the other spouse does not say, "I love you." Upon further investigation I have discovered that the spouse's lack of expression is not always the dilemma. Sometimes the problem is the lack of adequate articulation.

Tracey was upset that her husband Martin wouldn't woo her with his words. She complained that he never truly expressed how he felt for her. Well, this wasn't the case at all.

Martin would tell Tracey that he loved her, just not in the powerful and profuse way that she desired. After hearing Martin's heart for his wife, I explained that every man does not have an arsenal of words at their disposal. If she wanted her heart melted and her knees weakened she would have to be patient. Martin explained that his quest was to become more prolific with his words. However, it just hadn't manifested to the point that she liked. At the conclusion of our counseling session, I gave them two phrases that keep couples together in the holy state of matrimony, "Thank you" and "I'm sorry." These phrases hold more marriages together than saying, "I love you." If you say I'm sorry and thank you when necessary, your marriage will stand the test of time.

Let's recap. Be patient with your spouse in the areas of their actions, attitudes and articulation. This can allow your marriage to flourish and your spouse to appreciate you more.

## PATIENCE THROUGH PAIN

As I began this portion of the book I received a disturbing e-mail. The e-mail was from a young lady reaching out for help concerning her marriage and in particular, her husband. In the midst of her correspondence this lady wrote and I quote, "At this point I do not know if I can bear patience to wait to see if there will even be a result."

To this lady and to others like her, I say hold on—change is coming. True love bears all things because of patience. Look at what the Apostle Paul wrote in Scripture.

> And let us not be weary in well doing: for in due season we shall reap, if we faint not.
>
> —GALATIANS 6:9, KJV

This text holds the key to making it through your pain. Whatever you do, don't focus on your pain—focus on your promise. The promise from the Word of God is you will reap if you do not faint or give up.

A perfect example of this principle is found in the process of pregnancy. When women are going through pregnancy they are forced to carry excessive weight and all sorts of changes can occur in their bodies. My wife complained of discomfort many nights, and encountered countless mornings of sickness. However, in the midst of all this, Andrea was given a party, not a pity party, it was a party for her promise—a baby shower. Women sat and celebrated the expected child through the sharing of gifts. No one at the party was concerned with the pains of pregnancy, just the promise of the child that was coming.

Allow another example:

My father tells a story of a time when he was a child riding his bicycle. As the story goes, a car struck him so hard, the impact broke his leg. A doctor set my father's leg in a cast and told him that in six weeks he'd be able to walk, run and even ride his bike again.

Once my father was back in the neighborhood his friends were concerned and asked all sorts of questions about his obvious pain. He spent a moment talking about his pain, then immediately, he told his friends about the promise the doctor had given. The promise was in six weeks he would not only walk again or run again, but that he would be riding his bike again. And that promise came to fruition.

My friend, you may be experiencing some rough roads in your marriage. You might even be in a situation where your best days seem to be behind you. If so, allow love to carry you through. Pray to your heavenly Father and allow Him to give you a promise. In spite of the circumstances, get a grip on patience with bulldog tenacity, and you will see better days ahead. Now, that's a promise!

A man stood before a judge in the courtroom to receive sentencing for the crime he committed. The judge read the man's offences and pronounced his fifteen-year sentence in the state prison. In disbelief, the man protested. He said to the judge, "There's no way I can do fifteen years in the state prison." The judge then asked the man, "Can you do one day?" The man in a calm manner replied, "Well yes, I can do one day." The judge looked the man in his eyes and finalized the discussion by saying, "Good! For the next fifteen years, do one day at a time."

At times you may feel you're unable to face certain things.

However, do one day at a time and the problem won't seem so great.

You have taken your problem to God. Yet, you are facing the situation and feel that God has not heard your prayer or worse, He is ignoring your request for relief. I submit to you that God is not ignoring you. As a matter of fact, God is providing you with strength to endure. He gives resources like this book to help you face present problems and push forward to your future. We ask God for the blessing. What's more important to God is not the blessing that you receive, but the lesson you learn from your present condition.

Your marriage and your spouse deserve all that you can give. So, through God's kind of love, give patience. Give your spouse the kind of patience that seeks for progress not perfection. Give your spouse patience on purpose. Give your spouse the kind of patience that brings pleasure. Give your spouse the kind of patience that endures pain. After all, this is the kind of patience God has given you.

# two

# BE KIND—REWIND

*Love Is Kind*
*1 Corinthians 13:4*

YOUNG LOVE IS THE greatest! Who can deny the veracity of the previous statement? Young love does not refer to the age of the couple; it is a reference point of the time the love first occurs in the relationship between a man and woman. Every joke your spouse tells is funny and every idea your spouse has is a brilliant one. Well, just about every idea. I can recall I had some pretty crazy ideas at the beginning of my marriage, but you get the point.

Your favorite songs were songs you heard together, your favorite places were just that, favorite, because you would go together. Ahh! Young love is so nostalgic—so intoxicating. And then one day it happens! The young love grows so old it can collect social security. Your love festival is on its way to a funeral. The love you discovered in spring has now taken root in bitter cold winter.

You know what? Just as some people live in the hot state of Texas or the cold state of Alaska, there are those who live in the state of anger or depression. If this describes you, it doesn't have to be that way. It is possible to recapture the love you once had. Your marriage doesn't have to be reduced to the mundane, or even worse, mutiny between you and your spouse. Allow the following illustration to explain my point.

Years ago, when movie rental stores carried movies on videotapes, there was a sticker placed on each one, "Be Kind—

Rewind." This sticker was instructing everyone who rented movies to rewind the tape so that the movie would start at the beginning for the next customer. It wouldn't be right for a person to rent a movie, put the tape in the player and see the movie at its ending first.

Having this understanding, many marriages suffer because couples only see the relationship in its current state. The children aren't behaving right, the bills begin to stack up and schedules are so crazy—you don't know if you're coming or going. As frustrations mount, you used to see your spouse in a good light, but now you just want to turn the light off.

How do you rekindle the love? How do you stay connected to your spouse in the midst of your own personal World War? It's simple! Be kind to each other. When you are kind to your spouse it causes them to remember why they married you. And, when you are kind, the picture of your life rewinds and you both remember what's most important; your happiness together.

> And be ye kind one to another, tenderhearted,
> forgiving one another, even as God for Christ's sake
> hath forgiven you.
> —EPHESIANS 4:32, KJV

The love that you have for your spouse should always compel you to be kind. Am I suggesting that you walk around all day never saying or doing the wrong thing? Am I suggesting that your day be filled with whistling and bluebirds on your shoulder? Of course not! In reality we will say or do the wrong thing to our spouse at some point. However, when you are kind you'll make an assertive effort to right any wrongs.

Consider the following quote:

> I expect to pass through this life but once; therefore,
> if there be any kindness I can show or any good
> thing that I can do for any fellow being, let me do it
> now, not defer, or neglect it, for I shall not pass this
> way again.[1]
>
> —ANONYMOUS

Your spouse should come to expect kindness from you because you are motivated by love. Kindness shouldn't only be extended when you desire something from each other. Kindness shouldn't be seen only when you are being sexually intimate with one another.

Think about it! Why do we tend to be kind when we are seeking to have sex with our spouse? I'll tell you why! When we are kind it mentally rewinds us to a time when our love was young, consequently putting us in the mood for love. No one in their right mind goes to their spouse demanding to make love or being mean right before the moment. No, we have enough mule sense to know that doesn't work.

> And now, here's what I'm going to do: I'm going to
> start all over again. I'm taking her back out into the
> wilderness where we had our first date, and I'll court
> her. I'll give her bouquets of roses. I'll turn Heart-
> break Valley into Acres of Hope. She'll respond like
> she did as a young girl, those days when she was
> fresh out of Egypt.
>
> —HOSEA 2:14–15, THE MESSAGE

The man of this scripture understood the heart of this chapter. If he wanted his wife to respond correctly, he had to capture her heart by turning her heartbreak valleys into acres of hope. He fully understood that issues of life had bombarded her world and she needed to be refreshed and taken back to where their love began. Some woman may need to know that her husband still finds her attractive.

Hosea's wife Gomer had returned to a life of prostitution (Hosea 3:1–3). Before we judge Gomer's actions, let's peer into her pain. Although Hosea lavished her with love, she felt inadequate. She was insecure, and couldn't believe that he could truly love a woman in her condition. However, the prophet declares, "I'll give her bouquets of roses." The roses remind her that despite the weight gain or the weights of life, she is still the apple of his eyes.

Keep in mind, kindness causes your spouse to go back and revisit the love you both had in the beginning. Inherently, we need to understand kindness better. There are three features to kindness that will be discussed in this chapter:

- The benefits of kindness
- The blessings of kindness
- The battles of kindness

## The Benefits of Kindness

Did you know with kindness comes benefits? Now there's a word we all like to hear, "benefits." The word *benefit* is defined as a favorable or helpful factor or circumstance that brings us advantage or profit. Therefore, being kind to your spouse is not only for them, but is for you as well. It is profitable in three ways.

Kindness makes you:

- Attractive
- Approachable
- Amiable

**Attractive—capable of attracting; interesting, pleasing or appealing**

In today's society we have become too focused on how we look externally when true beauty is discovered from within (ladies, I proceed with caution). Way too much money is spent on cosmetics and plastic surgery. I don't purport that plastic surgery strictly for frivolous beauty is wrong or right. I won't let where I stand on such subjects cloud the point that I'm making. My point is this; to possess beauty one must work on character more than features. If you truly want to stay attractive to your spouse, you don't have to spend loads of money on cosmetics or surgery. Just be kind and there will be a natural attraction.

> What matters is not your outer appearance—the styling of your hair, the jewelry you wear, the cut of your clothes—but your inner disposition. Cultivate inner beauty, the gentle, gracious kind that God delights in. The holy women of old were beautiful before God that way, and were good, loyal wives to their husbands.
>
> —1 PETER 3:4–5, THE MESSAGE

Think back to before you were married. On your first date chances are you were very kind. Mister, you probably held the door open for her. More than likely, you complimented her on how she was dressed and said nice things about her hair. Ma'am, you probably listened attentively to what was on his heart (even if it didn't interest you). Chances are you told him how handsome he looked and commented on how good he smelled. If this was the case, if you did these things to get your spouse, you must know, these things should continue in order to keep your spouse. Whether you know it or not, these acts of kindness made you attractive and it's kindness that keeps you attractive.

When you are attractive to your spouse this segues to being approachable.

**Approachable—friendly; easy to talk to**

When you are kind it isn't a secret. There is no such thing as undercover kindness. However, you can do acts of kindness without others knowing it. Also, you can do acts of kindness just to act as if you're kind. However, when you are genuinely kind it is extremely difficult, next to impossible to keep it hidden.

My father often says, "If you're happy, make sure you tell your face." You can be the nicest person around and possess tremendous skills, but no one will know it if you have a mean countenance. Being approachable is a byproduct of kindness and is paramount in a marriage.

Your spouse needs to feel and ultimately know that they can approach you about any and everything.

I have a friend who was experiencing some turmoil in his marriage. He told me that his wife and he were continually arguing about other women approaching him in public settings and having casual conversations. He went on to say that his wife couldn't understand why these women would approach him. Through discernment of the Holy Spirit, I told him the problem wasn't that women approached him. The problem, according to his words, was that his wife couldn't understand why these women would approach him. In essence, how he conducted himself publicly wasn't how he conducted himself privately.

I instructed him to evaluate his behavior at home. In others words, be kind. I said, "If you are kind to your wife, she will understand why other women approach you."

Being approachable has everything to do with how we present ourselves. People watch how you look and they listen to not only what you say, but also how you say, what you say. They do this on the basis of discovering whether or not you're an approachable person. The person who knows you best is your spouse. If you're approachable, your spouse will reveal it to you. If your spouse never brings their concerns to you, you might have a problem displaying kindness.

Jesus asked His disciples, "Who do men say that I, the Son of Man, am?" (Matt. 16:13, NKJV). Then He asked them, "Who do you say that I am?" (v. 15, NKJV). The point is, people are going to have all sorts of opinions about who you are and most of them are not accurate, because your public persona is not always your private persona. The most accurate assessment of your kindness is seen through the eyes of your spouse.

Finally, being approachable means being gentle. When you know your spouse has had a difficult day, walk over to them, place your arms around them and with soft words say, "I love you and I'm here for you if you want to talk." If they choose to share what's bothering them, listen, not to give answers, not to solve problems, just listen. This goes a long way in a relationship. Your union to one another is being strengthened, and because you are approachable it reveals the best part about you to your partner.

You are amiable.

### Amiable—friendly; courteous and easygoing

In my first book *Marriage Matters: For Better or for Worse*, I discuss how your spouse is given by God to be your best friend. However, this friendship doesn't develop without you being friendly. Love causes you to be kind, and kindness manifests a congenial character within you.

Being an amiable person brings out an intrinsic value that says, "I care about my spouse's well being." You're not easily provoked into arguments. You are careful not to say or do things that will in anyway jeopardize your spouse's development as a person.

As a friend your spouse should draw strength from your presence that carries over to times when you are absent. To make sure that this is the case, speak with your spouse and discover if they see you in this manner. If your spouse doesn't feel your strength in their corner, encourage your partner not just with words, but with your actions. Let them know how much you desire their success in every area of their life. This may mean taking on some of their responsibilities—granting them time to recharge. You may have to perform a duty that will allow them room to succeed. If your spouse is in school, the childcare responsibilities may lie mainly with you. Show your partner that true success is not found in what they do, it's found in who they are becoming and as far as you're concerned, you are well pleased with them.

> Suppose one of you went to your friend's house at midnight and said to him, "Friend, loan me three loaves of bread."
>
> —Luke 11:5, ncv

Another important concept to consider about friendship is that you are willing to be imposed upon. Husbands and wives are placed in positions to be there for each other at all times.

Imagine you on your way home from a hard day of work. As you're driving all you can think of is getting home and unwinding. Suddenly, you get a call from your spouse asking if you can stop at the Wal-Mart store to pick up something they need. The very thought of standing in long lines to purchase the item causes your body to cry out for relief. However, because you are not just married, your spouse is your friend, you push your way through and bring home what your spouse desires.

This is what it means to be a friend. You are willing to go the extra mile for your friend and you don't make them feel bad for it. Sometimes we find ourselves going to great lengths for people outside of our homes, then when it comes to doing things for our spouse we complain. This should not be! Whatever we are willing to do for others, we should go twice as far or put forth twice the effort for our spouse.

> Some friends may ruin you, but a real friend will be more loyal than a brother.
>
> —PROVERBS 18:24, NCV

Above all else, being a friend to your spouse is a commitment of loyalty. Infidelity is out of the question (this topic is discussed in Chapter 10). As I stated earlier you are careful not to cause harm to your spouse. Therefore, sexual indiscretion with another person is something you would never succumb to because you would never allow yourself or anyone else to harm them. As you consider loyalty and friendship take a look at the subsequent quote.

> Everyone wants friends. They make us happy. They make life interesting and fun and profitable for us. They share our tastes, our desires, our sense of humor. And on a deeper level, friends help us become better human beings. The virtues demanded in real friendship—qualities such as honesty, trust, kindness, and generosity—all help us grow in a moral sense. The best of friends try to make each other better people. They lift each other up.[2]
>
> —WILLIAM J. BENNETT

This quote culminates the point I would like to make about the benefits of kindness. Through the benefits of kindness you become attractive, approachable and amiable. If these qualities are found within your marriage, both you and your spouse will become better people.

## The Blessings of Kindness

> Blessed are the merciful: for they shall obtain mercy.
>
> —Matthew 5:7, kjv

This scripture comes from the most famous teaching of Jesus Christ. In this teaching, the people were instructed how to receive God's blessings.

There are those who think in order to obtain a blessing from God they have to do something great, like having a great church attendance streak. One could consider these folks the Cal Ripken Jr.'s of church (Google for his accomplishment). Perhaps they want to be great philanthropists like Warren Buffet when it comes to giving tithes. No doubt, these would be great accomplishments, but it's not needful in order to receive a blessing from God. All that is required is to show mercy. And mercy is synonymous with kindness.

Being kindhearted is a mandate when it comes to being married. Mercy is being warm and soft, not cold and harsh with your spouse. The world and all it has to offer is hard enough without your spouse having to come home and receive the same treatment from you.

In Matthew 5, the Lord pronounced that when you show mercy you will be blessed. This word *blessed* means to make happy; to cause to prosper. In essence the Lord is saying, when things aren't going right in your marriage, even if your spouse is not doing right, He'll make you happy. When you think you can't go further, the joy of the Lord will become your strength.

God commanded His servant Hosea to go get his wife and show mercy to her even in her unfaithfulness.

> Then God ordered me, "Start all over: Love your wife again, your wife who's in bed with her latest boyfriend, your cheating wife. Love her the way I, God, love the Israelite people, even as they flirt and party with every god that takes their fancy." I did it. I paid good money to get her back. It cost me the price of a slave. Then I told her, "From now on you're living with me. No more whoring, no more sleeping around. You're living with me and I'm living with you."
>
> —HOSEA 3:1–3, THE MESSAGE

My friend, it's hard to imagine having to go through this kind of ordeal. However, you need to know that the Lord promises His blessings to those who are kind. If you find yourself in a situation like Hosea where your spouse has been unfaithful, let the Lord fight your battles and you receive His blessings.

As you trust the Lord with all your heart and don't try to figure out how He will work it out, He will give you His power and He will make your way prosperous.

## THE BATTLES OF KINDNESS

We have been discussing how kindness grants you benefits and God's blessings, but make no mistake about it, kindness also has battles. There are four enemies that wage war on kindness, two that are overt and two that are covert. These enemies are kindness killers. In essence they keep you from being kind to your spouse.

These enemies are:

- Unforgiveness
- Ungratefulness
- Familiarity
- Fatigue

**The overt enemies**

*Unforgiveness—not forgiving; ingratitude*

In life we often say, nobody's perfect. If we know this, why do we get so upset when our spouse makes mistakes? Loving your spouse through the attribute of kindness means that you remain ready to forgive them for infractions they might commit.

When we commit sin against God or transgress against others, God stands ready to forgive us. God doesn't forgive us after He's had time to think it over. He doesn't require us to prove that we come with a broken heart. He stands ready to grant forgiveness to all who seek His rest and restoration. God's forgiveness is granted immediately.

> But if we confess our sins, he will forgive our sins, because we can trust God to do what is right. He will cleanse us from all the wrongs we have done.
> —1 JOHN 1:9, NCV

The reason God extends forgiveness right away is because He knows that we have work to do in His kingdom. We are unable to advance God's kingdom if we are filled with guilt. Sin separates us from God, and we are reluctant to come to Him if we have sin operating in our lives.

This fact holds true in marriage. When couples are hesitant to forgive, the kingdom of their marriage suffers. Operating in the office of husband and wife is difficult enough without adding that your spouse has not forgiven you. Unforgiveness restricts our movement, and the relationship is broken. When you feel that your spouse doesn't see you right it becomes difficult to act right.

More importantly, if you are harboring unforgiveness in your heart towards your spouse you'll find it difficult to be kind and express your true love.

Unforgiveness is an overt enemy to kindness because although it may be hidden from your partner, it's not hidden from you. You know when you haven't forgiven your spouse of an offence. Therefore, you should give the offence to God in prayer and extend forgiveness to your spouse. After all, forgiving is, "for" "giving." If you keep forgiveness to yourself, you misappropriate its meaning.

*Ungratefulness—not thankful or appreciative*
This kindness killer is one we really need to pay attention to because it can cause serious strife and division in the marital union. I have seen cases where couples have split due to materialism.

Always remember to appreciate where you are in life. Andrea and I throughout our years of being married have known people who have had both great wealth and possessions. We have always appreciated what God was doing in the lives of other people. Even when the people have so much more than us, our mantra is what God has for us it is for us. Even more, what God has given us is far greater than we deserve.

This kind of attitude keeps us appreciative of what we have and doesn't add undue stress to our lives. When you are ungrateful it becomes extremely hard to be kind. It's hard to be kind because dissatisfaction breeds displeasure.

The cycle of materialism always ends in some form of addiction. What we thought would free us ends

up enslaving us. If we are trapped in materialism,
we never own things; they own us.[3]

—STEPHEN ARTERBURN

If you or your spouse is always chasing worldly possessions
you lose focus on what matters most and that is celebrating
your marriage. Ungratefulness can move you right out of the
will of God for your life. This is what happened in the case of
the Prodigal Son (Luke15:11–24). His ungratefulness left him
destitute and ashamed.

Whatever you do don't allow ungratefulness to kill your
kindness.

### The covert enemies

*Familiarity—close acquaintance with or knowledge of
something or someone*

Is it possible to love someone and treat them with contempt?
Unfortunately, the answer is yes. The reason being is we work
so hard outside the house to fit into social norms at our place of
business and in the community at large. When we come home
we can be physically and mentally drained. Even still, we need
to leave our work in the office not our kindness. When we come
home to unwind, the goal is still to rewind our relationship
with our spouse to the point where we keep our love alive.

Familiarity is a covert enemy to kindness because without
knowing it, we can take our spouse for granted based on closeness. Therefore, we don't try to impress them at all.

I read the following anecdotes and decided that they were
examples of how familiarity can creep into a marriage and
cause us not to be kind and show our partner love.

A woman sat down on the couch with her husband
as he was flipping through channels. She asked in a

pleasant voice, "What's on TV?" Without hesitation he responded, "Dust."

A man returned home from work at night, when his wife demanded that he take her someplace expensive...he took her to the gas station.

A man asked his wife, "Where do you want to go for our anniversary?" It warmed his heart to see her face melt in sweet appreciation. "Somewhere I haven't been in a long time!" She said. So he suggested, "How about the kitchen?"

Although, every tale showed the man being unkind we know that women can be just as harsh.

The point is this: just because you are familiar with one another, don't be any less kind to each other. In fact, go out of your way to ensure that you're being as kind to your spouse as you are to anyone else. Doing this shows your spouse respect and it keeps the love alive in your marriage.

*Fatigue—extreme tiredness or weariness resulting from physical or mental activity*

Like familiarity, fatigue is a covert enemy to kindness. Fatigue kills your kindness because a weary soul can cause a cranky disposition. If you're not cognizant, you can go days without being nice and not even know it.

If you're not getting the proper rest, fatigue can give way to stress. I know there are times when getting enough sleep can seem to be an event that occurs in a distant galaxy. However, you must get what you can and remain kind in the process.

Again, a lack of sleep can give way to stress, but take note that stress is normal. It's how your body responds to events that make you feel threatened or overwhelmed. Long-term stress can even rewire the brain, leaving you more vulnerable to anxiety and depression.

The following can cause stress and ultimately kill kindness:

- Death of a loved one
- Pregnancy or children
- Major purchases
- Holidays
- Work or school demands

When your body is fatigued you have a tendency to complain about not getting the rest required to function throughout a normal day. This in turn can cause you to be cranky. When you are cranky, you are less likely to be loving and kind. Love has a way of growing old if you let it. In order to keep our love fresh we must remember the benefits of kindness, the blessings of kindness, and never forget the battles of kindness. Take care not to lose your kindness because it is very vital in stimulating the love that your partner has for you.

"Be kind—rewind!"

# three

# COMMUNITY of UNITY

*Love Is Not Jealous*
*1 Corinthians 13:4*

With all lowliness and meekness, with longsuffering, forbearing one another in love; Endeavouring to keep the *unity* of the Spirit in the bond of peace.
—EPHESIANS 4:2–3, KJV, EMPHASIS ADDED

IN MY YEARS OF being married I have learned a few things, some good and some bad. I have learned never to tell Andrea that I can do what she does around the house. That is declaring war! It doesn't matter if it's true or not, if she ever thought I felt that way, oh boy...it would be like an episode of Jerry Springer. However, a good lesson for me has been to laugh at myself and at Andrea. In other words, I shouldn't take everything that happens between us in marriage so seriously.

Out of the myriad of lessons about marriage, one thing stands out the most. Marriage should be a "Community of Unity." When couples share the concept of a community of unity it keeps their marriage thriving and moving in the right direction. Having this community of unity means you stand with one another and encourage each other to succeed.

As simple as this might sound, many marriages falter because couples work in individual careers trying to succeed without the proper encouragement from their spouse. Many find their encouragement outside of the marital union, from co-workers or those interested in the same field of study.

Even more discouraging, couples can secretly harbor feelings of disdain or jealousy over their spouse's success. Normally, this kind of jealousy occurs through fear of losing that person. In actuality, you can become afraid that your spouse's success is pulling them away from you.

Jealousy over your spouse's success is demonically influenced and must be recognized and broken immediately. The most effective way to break the spirit of jealously or ensure that you never succumb to it is through prayer. There must also be an understanding that complementing each other makes the marriage complete. *Complementing* is not to be confused with *complimenting*. Complement means to come together and compliment means to say nice words.

## COMPLEMENT—DON'T COMPETE

Getting jealous when your spouse excels in life is ludicrous. When your spouse succeeds, you succeed.

I always had trouble with the concept of people separating because one spouse felt insignificant due to their counterpart's success. We see this with Hollywood couples all the time. They get married knowing that either both or at least one of them are successful. Suddenly, months later we are subject to the tabloids magnifying their messy break up.

Unfortunately, this same business is conducted in some Christian marriages. It would be great if everyone realized that marriage means two people should exist in a community of unity. Therefore, it shouldn't matter who brings home the bigger paycheck. One career shouldn't be seen as greater or lesser than the other. You're in the marriage to complement one another, not to compete.

Your marriage will experience tremendous unity when you can rely on one another for support. Even if you aren't interested in what your spouse does, you should be interested in your spouse. This being said, getting involved with what your spouse likes and standing with them goes a very long way in creating a community of unity within your marriage.

When your spouse knows that they have your full support and you are enthusiastic about their success, it causes them to love and value you more. Often times, Satan can cause division in marriages because one spouse doesn't feel the encouragement from the other spouse. Love is not jealous. Love desires to see others move forward (especially our spouse).

People can confuse jealously with love. I've heard it said that a person must really be in love when they exhibit jealousy. This is not true. We need to know that jealousy is not a sign of love, but rather, a major unity neutralizer. Although jealousy can have its beginning in a love relationship, it can lead to detriment. Jealousy is associated with emotions such as fear, anxiety, insecurity, anger, sadness and disgust which can ultimately spell danger.

If jealousy is not put in check it can lead to envy. Envy evolves from jealousy. Let's differentiate between the two:

- Jealousy—you want what someone else has.
- Envy—you don't necessarily want what someone else has; *you just don't want them to have it.*

More will be discussed on jealousy in Chapter 13.

When it comes to your marriage, remember that you are there to complement each other. If you and your spouse are competing with each other, your marriage is destined to fail.

> And any city or *family* that is divided against itself
> will not continue.
> —MATTHEW 12:25, NCV, EMPHASIS ADDED

## THE THREE COMPONENTS OF UNITY

Upon getting married, my wife and I decided that whatever we did we wanted to be in agreement with each other. Now thirteen years later, we still enjoy much fulfillment, and unity has been the key.

Unity is not something that comes easy in any relationship. However, to obtain it, a relationship must have three components: harmony, diversity, and maturity.

### Harmony

When you love your spouse you seek to become harmonious. Being in harmony is being congenial. Love is not jealous of its mate; you are not at war with your spouse. It's a sad commentary, but I know of couples who cannot be in the same room for a long time without ending a discussion in disagreement.

A certain couple would constantly ask Andrea and me to spend some evenings with them. However, not long into an evening this couple would begin arguing about anything. Once, Andrea became uncomfortable and asked if they wanted to be alone to work out their disagreements. The wife responded that our presence kept them from fighting. Imagine that! They bickered so much, they didn't consider that fighting. Later we discovered that having our company was their way of avoiding being alone. This couple was in desperate need of harmony within their marriage.

When you have harmony in your marriage you want to be around your spouse. Like a combination of musical notes that complement each other; together you produce a sound that others enjoy hearing. My wife and I endeavor to live such lives that when you think of me you think of her and vice versa.

The Bible records the times and works of a particular couple. They were with such an accord that when you thought of one you thought of the other. They were Aquila and Priscilla.

This couple worked together as tentmakers (Acts 18:2–3). As a team they instructed those who God used to preach the gospel in the Christian faith (Acts 18:24–26), and they assisted Paul in his public ministry. Paul even thanked them for risking their lives for him (Romans 16:3–4). I am convinced of their harmony by their exploits, but at the very mentions of their names, I sense togetherness—Aquila and Priscilla.

It's beautiful when couples display harmony, and harmony is at its best when there is diversity.

### Diversity

It's impossible for jealousy to exist within unity. For that reason unity must be explained within the context of diversity. In marriage, we must reach for harmony but not at the expense of diversity. Harmony doesn't mean uniformity in the sense that the couple must be identical. Yet, they find their two identities are complementary for unity.

My wife has taught me to appreciate classical music. When you are witnessing a really good symphony it has its mixture of wind, percussion and string instruments. One instrumental section is no more important than the next; all are needed to produce the desired symphonic sound.

Paul spoke on the importance of diversity when he wrote a letter to a church in Corinth. Consider what part of his letter reads:

> I want you to think about how all this makes you
> more significant, not less. A body isn't just a single

> part blown up into something huge. It's all the
> *different-but-similar* parts arranged and functioning
> together.... For no matter how significant you are, it
> is only because of what you are a part of.
>
> —1 Corinthians 12:14, 19, the message
> emphasis added

Being different is important. However, being different is never to be confused with being better or worse. Diversity is extremely fundamental when it comes to having a community of unity. This must be stated because the very word *community* means having things in common.

My neighborhood is racially mixed. Although diverse, what we all share in common is our community and we take great pride in keeping it clean and safe. It is asinine for one group of people to think of themselves better or worse than the others because we all live in the same community.

To truly operate in your diversity you must appreciate the fact that you are different. You may not approach every situation the same way, but as the axiom states, two heads are better than one.

Once there was a duck who was confused about who he was and what talent he possessed. Therefore, Mister Duck decided to attend the boot camp for talented animals. When he arrived, the Sergeant in charge of the boot camp asked Mister Duck what talent he would like to enlist in.

Mister Duck said, "I would like to..." and before he could finish his statement a roadrunner came racing by so fast Mister Duck almost toppled over. Impressed with the roadrunner's speed Mister Duck said, "I want to run like the roadrunner." He tried but his huge feet prevented him. A discouraged Mister Duck returned to the Sergeant of the boot camp.

Again, the Sergeant asked Mister Duck what talent interested him. Mister Duck said, "I would like to..." His attention was diverted when he saw a squirrel climbing trees and leaping from branch to branch. Mister Duck shouted, "I want to climb trees like the squirrel." As he ran off, with those huge flapping feet, he discovered that he couldn't climb trees either. Once again he returned disappointed.

Again, the Sergeant enquired of Mister Duck's talent aspirations. As before, Mister Duck exclaimed, "I would like to..." And just then something caught Mister Duck's eye. It was an eagle soaring in the sky. Mister Duck thought to himself, surely I can soar like the eagle. After all I have wings, too.

With much force and power Mister Duck began flapping his wings. As he reached a certain altitude his efforts were thwarted, because unlike the eagle, Mister Duck couldn't fly too high. However, when Mister Duck came down he landed in a pond.

Without trying Mister Duck's big webbed feet allowed him to swim with the grace of a swan. Suddenly, the roadrunner, the squirrel and the eagle stopped to watch Mister Duck swim. The Sergeant of the Animal Boot Camp smiled and said, "Mister Duck, I think you've found your talent."

> Now there are diversities of gifts, but the same Spirit.
> —1 CORINTHIANS 12:4, KJV

Invariably you are different from your spouse and possess a different set of skills, but it is God's Spirit that will enable you both to flow together smoothly. When you can appreciate diversity and not seek conformity, a community of unity will remain within your marriage. Love won't allow you to become jealous of what your spouse has or is able to accomplish. Through love you appreciate each other's diversities.

## Maturity

> That we henceforth *be no more children*...But
> speaking the truth in love, *may grow up* into him in
> all things, which is the head, even Christ.
> —EPHESIANS 4:14–15, KJV, EMPHASIS ADDED

Anyone who is jealous of their spouse for any reason shows signs of immaturity. If marriage is going to work it should go without saying, but I'll say it just in case, the couple must be mature.

Too often, I have counseled couples who resemble Little Rascals. When I say Little Rascals I'm speaking of the popular series that started running on television in the 1950's. These were kids who often dressed up like adults and in some cases look like little adults, but got in all kinds of big trouble. After all, they were just kids. Some couples dress like adults and look like adults, but behave like kids.

When you are mature you are involved in the progress of your home and family. This takes work from both partners. Allow this example to explain my point.

My father and mother stayed in a hotel in Austin, Texas. While in their room my father decided to make some coffee. Having all the necessary ingredients for the coffee was not enough for him to enjoy his usual cup.

First, he had to plug the coffee maker into the electrical outlet. Then he had to flip the power switch. After the coffee brewed, he was able to enjoy his cup of Joe. As he went back for his customary second cup, he noticed that the coffee maker was not on, and asked my mother had she turned it off. When she expressed that she hadn't, he explored the situation and discovered that the coffee maker automatically shut off.

When you enter marriage it is not enough to simply say we

are old enough to marry; you must be mature enough to marry. Being mature means that you are able to handle life's setbacks together and not fall apart. When tough times come into your marriage, stay plugged in and turned on. Most importantly, don't allow the ordinary trifles of married life to cause you to automatically shut off.

Maturity within a couple usually spells security within a marriage.

You must complement, not compete, with your spouse through consistent support. Jealousy will be expelled when you understand and apply the components of harmony, diversity and maturity. By this, your marriage will be guaranteed a community of unity.

# four

# WHO'S the MAN? NO!
# WHO'S the WOMAN?

*Love Does Not Brag*
*1 Corinthians 13:4*

I'VE READ 1 CORINTHIANS 13 numerous times, and one point that has eluded me is, love does not brag.

I understood why the writer wrote love is patient, love is kind, love is not jealous, but I must admit, I was quite taken when I read, love does not brag. Is it really necessary to include this admonishment in the text? Do husbands and wives really brag to each other? I regret to report, the answer is yes.

Couples brag to gain the favor of others and the respect of their spouse. Bragging can take on many shapes and colors. However, it's always easy to identify. Its shape or color all depends on who is talking, but no matter who is speaking you know bragging when you hear it.

Bragging is not appreciated in any setting. It certainly doesn't belong in a marriage where two people are joined together by God to make up a team.

> Let another man praise thee, and not thine own mouth; a stranger, and not thine own lips.
>
> —PROVERBS 27:2, KJV

## LET GO OF EGO

In too many households you have husbands asking the question, "Who's the man?" And no sooner than he can complete his braggadocios statement the wife responds, "No! Who's the woman?"

It is never a good thing to toot your own horn. However, couples tend to do this with one another. Normally, this is done to gain appreciation from your spouse.

We can begin to compare one another's responsibilities whether it is in or outside the house. We can say things like, "I do more than you" or "What I do has greater meaning." How about this one, "Who pays all the bills around here?" Usually, this kind of contest doesn't gain the respect of our spouse, but causes them to think that we're grandstanding. What needs to be recognized is that both individuals contribute and play an intricate role in the success of the marriage.

When you get married your ego needs to be checked at the door. When your spouse married you they wanted you, singular, one person. The problem with the ego is it carries too many people, me, myself and I.

A husband asked his wife braggingly, "Tell me, Dear, have you ever been in love before?" She thought a moment and replied, "No, Darling, I once respected a man for his great intelligence. I admired another for his remarkable courage. I was captivated by yet another for his good looks and charm. But with you, well, how else could you explain it, except love?"

Marriage has a unique way of keeping us in the right perspective. Somehow there's no room to get the big head. However, I will say, let us compliment our loved ones more. If we compliment them on their accomplishments they won't crave attention from us or others.

Ego shows up when we feel that no one is noticing what

we do. Your husband may not be the Head of State, making decisions that will affect the world. However, he is the Head of your household and the decisions he makes affect you. Your wife may not be some super model, but she is modeling good character and setting the right standards for your children. Not to mention, she looks good enough for you and that's what matters.

When we appreciate each other in marriage, ego is let go and bragging gives place to love.

## PREFER TO DEFER

Do not talk down about your spouse in order to make yourself look good to others. The purpose of being together as a couple is to make each other better. We gain more respect from other people when we prefer to defer to our spouse. Always place your spouse before or above yourself.

My wife has developed the hobby of taking photographs and placing them on DVDs accompanied by music for others to enjoy. Well, one day I was speaking with a relative of mine by phone. He was so excited to see Andrea's work. He also has developed an affinity when it comes to working with photos.

Well, as he began celebrating Andrea's creative bent, he commented on the great photography. Now to be honest, I had taken the pictures. Therefore, I told him so, but I quickly moved the conversation back to the work Andrea had done. After all, this was her time to shine and I felt tremendously proud that he had taken an interest in my wife's work. It would have been wrong to talk about myself and my accomplishments over what Andrea had done.

Unfortunately, I have witnessed people degrading their spouse while at the same time exalting themselves. There was a particular woman who always brought her husband up in conversations. She would tell everyone that her husband was slow grasping information, while saying she was rather witty and quite acquisitive for knowledge. The one thing that she didn't pick up was how truly uncomfortable she made others by demeaning her husband, which did nothing for her character either.

Again, the best thing is not to brag about your accomplishments. Let others tell about the good that you do. Love doesn't brag or boast on itself. Love concentrates on lifting others to their full potential.

> But, "If people want to brag, they should brag only about the Lord." It is not those who say they are good who are accepted but those the Lord thinks are good.
>
> —2 CORINTHIANS 10:17, NCV

When you love your spouse correctly, you won't deliberately embarrass them. In fact, you go out of your way to make sure that they are seen in an admirable light.

If your spouse is the subject of your jokes, just make sure they know you are kidding and not belittling them. I for one have been on the tail end of jokes at many social gatherings, and most of the time I'm the one telling the jokes. However, there are those times when I'm poking fun at Andrea; it's never demeaning or meant to cause harm. I always watch to make sure that she isn't bothered by my teasing.

I always want my wife to be respected. Accomplishing this is one of my life's goals. Although I know what people think of my wife is ultimately up to how she handles herself, I still do what I can to encourage her self-esteem. I didn't say inflate her ego, none of us needs that, but I want her to know that she is significant, especially in my eyes. Besides, when she looks good I look good and vice versa.

## MIRROR, MIRROR ON THE WALL

> This is what the LORD says: "The wise must not brag about their wisdom. The strong must not brag about their strength. The rich must not brag about their money. But if people want to brag, let them brag that they understand and know me. Let them brag that I am the LORD, and that I am kind and fair, and that I do things that are right on earth. This kind of bragging pleases me," says the LORD.
> —JEREMIAH 9:23–24, NCV

The final point to be made about bragging is if it continues to progress, you can become narcissistic—thinking that no one else can do a better job than you. You begin to believe that no one else looks better than you. Much like the witch in Disney's classic cartoon, *Snow White*, you'll find yourself talking into a mirror, asking who is the fairest of them all.

Like the witch, you'll have to talk to the mirror, because no one else can stand being around you.

Some wives complain that their husbands do no work around the house. However, when the husband does something the wife complains that it is not done right. The question becomes, is it not done right or is it not done the way she would do it? The same is to be said about the husband. Don't deride your wife because the way she chooses to handle bills is not according to your method. If the bills get paid, be satisfied.

Bragging tends to make a person feel that their way is not only the best way, it's the only way. And, bragging can cause self-centeredness. In a marriage you should be thinking of your spouse's needs. This is not to say that you ignore your own, just don't allow yourself to take center stage. The purpose of any mirror is to remind us that we're not perfect, that we don't have it all together. We are to look in the mirror to fix what we see (making improvements), not become fixated with what we see (making impressions).

The Bible tells us that we are to look in the mirror of God's Word to see who we should really resemble and that's Jesus.

> But we all, with open face beholding as in a glass the glory of the Lord, are changed into the same image from glory to glory, even as by the Spirit of the Lord.
>
> —2 CORINTHIANS 3:18, KJV

The point to be made in the previous scripture is that in order for us to reflect the right image and be the right person we must look into God's glass. The word *glass* in this scripture has the same meaning as mirror. When we look into God's mirror (the Bible) we don't see ourselves we see Jesus. Just like in the case of the witch, when she asked who was the fairest, the mirror didn't reflect the witch, it showed Snow White. There is only One who is pure and without sin. His name is Jesus!

When you see Jesus, when you look like Jesus, you can't help but love like Jesus. Remember, it is Jesus who makes us who we are, "The man" or "The woman."

So, the next time you see your husband or your wife smile and tell them, "Yeah! You're the man," or "You're the woman."

# five

# THE SECRET to MARRIAGE SUCCESS

*Love Is Not Proud*
*1 Corinthians 13:4*

I F YOU'RE MARRIED AND you're reading this book, chances are you would like to see your marriage succeed. If you're not married and you're reading this book, you're really smart; you get a head start on achieving a favorable marriage. Whoever you are, whatever category you fall into, this chapter will reveal what kills or keeps marriages.

It is God's desire that every marriage experience His good success. In order for your marriage to work it must line up with God's Word. Beware of what you consider success. Also be careful by which means you choose to accomplish a successful marriage.

Society has taught us that going up is equivalent to having success. However, when receiving God's success you must first go down.

When God first called His servant Abraham He told him to leave his family. God did this with the purpose of taking Abraham and Sarah someplace (Gen. 12:1). God calls every couple to come out from their relatives in order to take them somewhere in their marriage.

> Therefore shall a man leave his father and his mother, and shall cleave unto his wife: and they shall be one flesh.
>
> —GENESIS 2:24, KJV

God was taking Abraham and Sarah to a place of success in their marriage and on the road to this success they had to first travel down.

> And there was a famine in the land: and Abram went *down* into Egypt to sojourn there; for the famine was grievous in the land.
> —GENESIS 12:10, KJV, EMPHASIS ADDED

When God told them to travel this road to success, He knew they would experience famine. God allows us to experience trials in order to bring us to the place of humility. Humility in the Bible is associated with the direction of down. The Bible teaches, "Humble yourselves in the sight of the Lord, and he shall lift you up" (James 4:10). The reason the Lord has to lift you up is because humbling is a downward position.

Due to tough times Abraham went down. However, his going down was so that God could bring him up in a better lifestyle.

> And Abram went *up* out of Egypt, he, and his wife, and all that he had, and Lot with him, into the south. And Abram was very rich in cattle, in silver, and in gold.
> —GENESIS 13:1–2, KJV, EMPHASIS ADDED

God brought Abraham up and added to his life an abundance of wealth that he never knew. God desires to do the same for us and our marriage.

When you try to go up in your marriage without God the results can be disastrous. An example of this is found in the Devil himself.

Read the following account:

> How art thou fallen from heaven, O Lucifer, son of
> the morning! how art thou *cut down* to the ground,
> which didst weaken the nations! For thou hast said
> in thine heart, I will ascend into heaven, I will *exalt*
> my throne *above* the stars of God: I will sit also
> upon the mount of the congregation, in the sides
> of the north: I will *ascend above* the heights of the
> clouds; I will be like the most High. Yet thou shalt
> be brought *down* to hell, to the sides of the pit.
> —ISAIAH 14:12–14, KJV, EMPHASIS ADDED

In reading this account we see that the plan of Satan was to move himself up Heaven's corporate ladder, but God had to cut him down.

Jesus, who is to always be our example, gives us the right picture of how to obtain God's success.

> But made himself of no reputation, and took upon
> him the form of a servant, and was made in the
> likeness of men: And being found in fashion as a
> man, *he humbled himself,* and became obedient
> unto death, even the death of the cross. Wherefore
> *God also hath highly exalted him,* and given him a
> name which is *above* every name: That at the name
> of Jesus every knee should bow, of things in heaven,
> and things in earth, and things under the earth.
> —PHILIPPIANS 2:7–10, KJV, EMPHASIS ADDED

As Jesus chose to go down in humility through humanity, God decided to lift Him up by His deity.

In lieu of that, what needs to be stated is the devil takes us up if we allow him. Consider the following scriptures:

> Then the devil *taketh him up* into the holy city, and
> setteth him on a pinnacle of the temple.... Again,
> the devil *taketh him up* into an exceeding high
> mountain, and sheweth him all the kingdoms of the
> world, and the glory of them.
>                    —MATTHEW 4:5, 8, KJV, EMPHASIS ADDED

Do not allow the devil to take your marriage up. Trust God and His way and your marriage will not only go up, it will stay up. You will discover in this chapter that the way up with God is always down.

It is well documented that it takes love for God's kind of marriage to develop and blossom. If this is common knowledge, if it really is just that basic, then why do so many couples find themselves in marital counseling? I'm not knocking marital counseling. If you need it, get it. However, a lot of counseling could be curtailed if couples understood what kills marriages and what keeps marriages.

## MARRIAGE KILLER

The number one killer of marriage is pride. Pride, like a cancer, can devour the love within a union. I never will forget a billboard I read, "Anger gets you in trouble, but pride keeps you there." That simple and yet profound statement changed my life entirely. From that moment, I do whatever it takes to rid myself of this marriage killer.

Remember, in your marriage, whenever pride steps in, love steps out. It's virtually impossible for the two to occupy the same space. Pride stinks in the nostrils of God and I can't stand the smell of it either.

Pride causes us to have:

- Self-presentation
- Self-preservation
- Self-pretense

**Self-presentation**

People who suffer from self-presentation have to constantly introduce themselves in every scenario. No matter where they go the topic has to be about them. They think that the entire world only exists to revolve around or involve them.

Linda had complained that Jeff was becoming unbearable to live with. She said every conversation had to be about his job, his accomplishments, and his needs. If Linda tried to get a word in about her or the children, Jeff somehow turned the conversation back to himself. Arguments arose frequently in their home because Jeff refused to put a penny toward anything that didn't involve him directly. Things got so bad, Linda revealed that Jeff wouldn't pay for the children's school pictures because he wasn't in them.

Many may find this account humorous and may even scoff at someone like Jeff. However, pride has a way of disguising itself. If not careful, we can allow ourselves to get caught up in self-presentation. After all, Jeff didn't see anything wrong with the way he was behaving. This is how self-presentation looks. First, you don't see anything wrong with talking about yourself, and then you don't see anything but yourself.

A man who was experiencing financial hardship got angry with a friend who told him he had much to be thankful for. "Don't be absurd," he said. "What have I to be thankful for? I am thousands of dollars in debt and I can't pay my bills." His friend said, "Be thankful that you aren't one of your creditors."

Through the pride of self-presentation you can owe others and not even care because your focus is always on yourself. You could owe your spouse or your children your time. If you do, put it off no longer; go and pay your debt.

## Self-preservation

Self-preservation is something that we're all pre-wired with at birth. Innately we all look to protect ourselves from clear and present danger. However, with pride, this innate tendency can go too far. When you have self-preservation your primary goal is to protect "Me."

Sondra's pride causes her to think of herself excessively. She's an upper-level executive at her company, and has been married for three years. According to Sondra, her husband's job isn't a good one. Her salary is larger than his. She feels that he won't be able to keep up with her in corporate America. Therefore, she has been stashing money away in a secret account just for herself. Sondra reasons that this is for her future protection while all along she is destroying the trust in their marriage.

Kenneth forgets to do chores around the house all the time. When his wife calls to ask if he has done them, Kenneth says he has, because he doesn't want to face the music (arguments). When Kim gets home she discovers that Kenneth has done nothing and the music Kenneth didn't want to face initially, he dances to all night long.

The common thread in both these cases is the lies that often get told all in the name of self-preservation. Pride can tell you to protect yourself even at the expense of your marriage. If you think that lying to your mate can hurt your marriage, wait until you see what living a lie can do.

> When pride cometh, then cometh shame: but with the lowly is wisdom.
>
> —PROVERBS 11:2

**Self-pretense**

People who operate in self-pretense are great pretenders. They live pretending to be who they are not or act as if they possess things they really don't have. This can cause great strain on the marriage.

Alan works two jobs and is considering a third because his wife, Sharon, likes the finer things in life. Although they can't afford them, Alan strives to please her. Sharon works with friends who can afford to live lavishly. Therefore, she puts pressure on Alan by saying things like, "My friends' husbands buy them nice things. Why can't you buy me nice things?"

Alan, desiring to be a good husband, works to give Sharon her heart's desires. However, she has a heart problem, "Pride"! Sharon knows that they can barely afford to live at the level which they have been living, but her pride can't let her friends know. Consequently, she is jeopardizing her marriage to a good man just for the sake of appearing wealthy.

> Pride goeth before destruction, and an haughty spirit before a fall.
>
> —PROVERBS 16:18, KJV

Pride is a marriage killer! It needs to be identified then eliminated. Where pride remains, love can't stay. We need to always express our love for our spouse and this will usher us into the very spirit that keeps our marriage.

## MARRIAGE KEEPER

What will protect and preserve your marriage is humility. Humility is not a "me first" attitude, it's a "you first" attitude. Many have a problem with humility because somehow they feel that humility means thinking of you-less. This is not true.

Humility is not thinking of yourself as less (lowering your value or worth) it is thinking less of you and more of others. You become other people minded. Your mind is on what it takes to please your spouse.

> Whoever is your servant is the greatest among you. Whoever makes himself great will be made humble. Whoever makes himself humble will be made great.
>
> —MATTHEW 23:11–12, NCV

God takes us to higher levels in Him not to make us see ourselves bigger than we are, but to reveal that we are small and insignificant without Him. It's called putting things in proper perspective.

For our eleventh wedding anniversary, Andrea and I visited the Grand Canyon. I noticed as she and I were on level ground my thoughts were more on us and what we wanted to do next. As she and I scaled the mountains the higher we reached, my thoughts shifted from us and what we wanted to do next to God and what He wanted to do next.

This happened naturally, because the higher we climbed the mountains, the smaller everything appeared, (especially me). As we peered down the canyon we could see the Colorado River. We saw eagles as they would soar and swoop at ease. *My God*, is all I could think as I stood there gazing at God's creation, thanking Him for including me in His plan. I felt—well—I felt—humbled.

> Six days later, Jesus took Peter, James, and John, the brother of James, up on a high mountain by themselves.
>
> —MATTHEW 17:1, NCV

God will take you up with the purpose of saving your marriage through humility. It's through humility that you learn to say four of the most powerful words you will ever ask in your marriage, "Will you forgive me?"

## The Recipe for Apology

Too many marriages have been left in the carnage of broken promises, and filed in the category of "what could have been." These marriages have shot off with the passion and promise of lasting forever only to be found crushed under a mountain of mistakes and multiple misunderstandings.

Did these marriages have to fail? Better question, must the life of your marriage be cut short? The answer is unequivocally no as long as you do not allow pride to dominate your relationship.

It doesn't matter who you are or where you're from, if you are married, you and your spouse will have disagreements. These disagreements have a tendency to lead to arguments. If not an argument, there will be times when you offend your partner in some way. Therefore, the question becomes, when you have done something wrong, how do you handle it? Some couples try to seek refuge in their neutral corners. Some even go days without speaking, hoping that time only will heal the problem or right the wrongs.

For various reasons the previous remedies have proven to be ineffective. The proven solution to solving any marital spat or injustice is the proper apology. Before I go further let me say that pride will not permit you to apologize to your spouse. You must remember to love your spouse and since love is not proud, through humility, you can apologize for any wrong that you have committed.

Having said that, there is a recipe for an apology that if

followed properly, just about any situation can be rectified and your spouse will be left satisfied. Adhere to these five steps for an effective apology:

1. Recall
2. Responsibility
3. Regret
4. Restitution
5. Resolution

**Recall**

> Remember therefore from whence thou art fallen, and repent, and do the first works.
>
> —REVELATION 2:5, KJV

The first work in restoring your relationship is apologizing, and this can only be done through repentance. To repent means you think differently about the situation or how you handled the situation. The first step of recalling is going to your spouse and rationally discussing the problem. You cannot skip the first step. Recalling is imperative in the process of apologizing because it allows your spouse to see that your apology is for the right reason. In other words, you are making sure that you and your spouse are talking about the same thing.

This shows your spouse that you have thought things over and with their assistance you're willing to think things through. When you are able to discuss the situation without fighting it shows your maturity. Whenever my children are fighting amongst themselves and I hear it, as the adult, I step in and the first thing I need to know is what happened. In essence, I'm asking my children to recall the events that brought them to the point of fighting one another. If this method works for our children shouldn't it work for us?

When recalling, it is important that we monitor the tone of our voices not sounding harsh or condescending. Recalling must never be done while still angry. I heard someone say, "If you speak while you are angry, you'll make the best speech you'll ever regret." It is important to understand how you arrived at this point in your marriage so you don't repeat the same mistake.

Finally, when recalling, be specific in your discussion. When you acknowledge your offence don't generalize by saying things like, "I'm sorry for getting you upset" you must be willing to express what you did to get them upset. This brings us to step two.

### Responsibility

> I will leave and return to my father and say to him, "Father, I have sinned against God and against you."
>
> —LUKE 15:18, NCV

This step is important because it says that you are ready to take responsibility for the role that you played in the conflict and you're not trying to offer excuses. When you accept responsibility for your wrong and apologize for the hurt that you caused, it allows your spouse the opportunity to let go of the pain.

Your partner's pain is fueled because all the blame is being placed on them. Release them of the burden of trying to deal with all the blame and you release them of the burden of carrying all the pain. Don't try to justify your actions. Remember this is supposed to be an apology. The apology should be about them and reassuring your spouse of the love that you have for them.

It doesn't matter if what you did was unintentional, you still caused harm and hurt. Therefore, you should seek to dispel all pain if possible. Don't avoid your responsibility, admit it. When you recognize and reveal your faults, pride is defeated and love wins again.

## Regret

> Abram said to Lot, "There should be no arguing between you and me, or between your herdsmen and mine, because we are brothers."
>
> —GENESIS 13:8, NCV

The third step of regret causes you to reflect on the entire situation. Through regret you should feel remorse. When you are truly regretful, you experience remorse. Remorse causes you to seek for personal change.

An example of this kind of remorse is found in the account of the patriarch in the Bible Abraham. Look at the following scripture.

> The LORD said to Abram, "Leave your country, your relatives, and your father's family, and go to the land I will show you."
>
> —GENESIS 12:1, NCV

Abraham, in spite God's instructions to leave his relatives, took his nephew Lot. After strife arose between Abraham and his nephew, Abraham began to feel regret for not obeying God. However, Abraham's regret moved him to remorse and he sought personal change. Abraham went to his nephew and told him that they must separate. This personal change got Abraham back in the Will of God.

Your personal change doesn't have to be separation from love ones; it can be separation from bad habits. Whatever it may be, don't wait any longer to get back into the Will of God. It's the Will of God that your marriage continues to flourish. Therefore, apologizing to your spouse for misdeeds is important.

Tell your spouse that you regret the incident, and ask for forgiveness. Explain to your spouse that you know your actions jeopardized peace in your marriage. Remember the key to regret is if you could do it over, you would do it differently.

## Restitution

> A quietly given gift soothes an irritable person; a heartfelt present cools a hot temper.
> —PROVERBS 21:14, THE MESSAGE

Whenever possible, when you apologize offer a gift. This is called your peace offering. In biblical times, the children of Israel gave God a peace offering. This offering represented three things:[1]

- The covering of sin;
- Forgiveness by God;
- The restoration of a right and meaningful relationship with God and life itself.

As it was then with God, so it is now with your spouse. When you have done wrong you need to come to your spouse with a peace offering. Your peace offering will help cover the wrong you committed thereby causing your spouse to forgive you and consequently, allow restoration in your relationship.

Keep in mind, with your gift the emphasis should not be on price. The gift could be a card, flowers or maybe even cooking a nice meal.

This being the case, you need to be cautioned, your gift does not substitute your apology it accompanies your apology. Many have tried to skip steps one through three and go straight to step four.

Your spouse won't accept your apology unless it's given in the right order. They might accept your gift, but the point of the gift is not to appease the situation. There must be recall, responsibility, and regret, along with your restitution or the apology won't be effective.

If you are in an automobile accident and the fault is on the other person, you look for their insurance company to pay restitution for the damages. The same should be done to amend offences in marriage.

Restitution says, I took time and thought about the situation and I'm offering this gift to let you know I care.

### Resolution

> So when you offer your gift to God at the altar, and you remember that your brother or sister has some-thing against you, leave your gift there at the altar. Go and make peace with that person, and then come and offer your gift.
>
> —MATTHEW 5:23–24, NCV

This scripture is profound in that God doesn't want you to make peace with Him if you have not attempted to make peace with your brother or sister or in the case of marriage, your spouse.

Resolution is the final step in the recipe for apology, but is also the most critical. Apologizing with meaning is striving to never commit the act again. You don't want to do the same things over and over again. Therefore, a resolution is in order.

Love always seeks peace. Peace is brought through the resolution.

Even if what brought on the conflict in your marriage was unintentional, or out of spite, both you and your spouse said some hurtful things. There must be an apology through humility. Your apology must include a plan to prevent the same conflict from reoccurring. Resolutions don't just happen—they happen on purpose.

Remember the secret to marriage success is to go down in humility. Don't allow the marriage killer (pride) to ruin your relationship. Release the marriage keeper (humility) and your marriage will overflow with God's abundance. If you ever run into a wall created through mistakes in your marriage, the recipe of apology will help you find a bridge allowing you and your spouse to pass on and continue growing.

# six

# WHERE IS the LOVE?

*Love Is Not Rude*
*1 Corinthians 13:5*

I WOULD LIKE TO BEGIN this chapter with a warning. Do not abuse what was meant to give you pleasure.

As I have stated on many occasions, we are in our marriage to complement our spouse and to bring them pleasure. We rely on them to give us feedback about whether we are accomplishing this goal. Therefore, do not take a great marriage for granted by constantly displaying rudeness.

At one point or another we have all been told that we have acted rude. Sometimes this admonishment is conveyed through our spouse. If the rudeness continues it could leave your spouse asking the question, Where is the love?

> Let us think about each other and help each other to show love and do good deeds.
> —HEBREWS 10:24, NCV

Love is not rude. Love considers your spouse's feelings, and will cause you to respect and esteem them. They in turn will look forward to talking with you and just being in your presence. If they don't enjoy your fellowship, there is a great possibility that you are rude.

Rudeness can stem from a person's character, but this doesn't mean that it cannot be corrected.

## A Crack in Character

I unequivocally believe that you were attracted to your spouse's character above anything else. Albeit, when people date (especially women), they notice things about their partner's character that they do not approve of. However, they move forward in the relationship expecting to change what is undesirable. This should never happen.

If we plan on purchasing an expensive vase and we notice a crack in it, we usually will not buy it. Well, the same treatment should be given to finding our partner for life. I'm not suggesting that we look for someone without imperfections; there is no such person. However, we should seek someone whose character is compatible with our own. Having compatible characteristics does not mean that you are just alike (who needs that!); it means you are agreeable and able to live in harmony.

The following passage really speaks on the heart and affect of character:

> Your character is who you truly are. It will affect how much you accomplish in this life. It will determine whether or not you are worth knowing. It will make or break every one of your relationships. Your character is instrumental in establishing how long you will be able to hold on to the fortune afforded you by hard work and good luck. Your character is the internal script that will determine your response to failure, success, mistreatment, and pain. It reaches into every facet of your life. It is more far-reaching than your talent, your education, your background, or your network of friends. These things can open

doors for you. Your character determines what happens once you pass through those doors.[1]

—ANDY STANLEY

Character is what a person has that makes them unique. It is how we can distinguish one person from another. Character has to do with a person's mental and moral makeup.

When dating, people tend to behave in all the right ways. Somehow after marriage, we stop trying to make a good impression on our mate. If we love them our desire should always be to impress them with the right attitude and good nature. I'm not talking about impressing them by performing tricks or some great feat; I'm speaking of impressing our love upon them by not being rude. We must correct the cracks in our character.

How do we correct our character?

First, we should take correction from our spouse. When they say something is rude, don't just blow it off with a "like it or lump it" attitude. Don't dismiss it by saying, "I'm just being me." Remember, we expect our spouse to please us, and we should go out of our way to please them.

> Fools think they are doing right, but the wise listen to advice.
>
> —PROVERBS 12:15, NCV

> Consider what I say; and the Lord give thee understanding in all things.
>
> —2 TIMOTHY 2:7, KJV

Second, we must want to change. Although some people are literally afraid of growth, we should embrace it. Do not settle for *growing old*; prefer *growing up*. Growing up means being willing to change. We change clothes, shoes, social environments, jobs, our physical appearance; everything about us changes. Why should we hold on to nasty or offensive behaviors that bother our spouse?

Finally, if we're going to correct our character, our desire should be for our spouse to see us in the right way. We should appreciate the fact that our spouse doesn't want to see us in a bad light and seize the moment to make mid-term corrections.

## MINOR FOXES, MAJOR FIXES

> Take us the foxes, the little foxes, that spoil the vines: for our vines have tender grapes.
> —SONG OF SOLOMON 2:15, KJV

In order to keep freshness in your marriage there must be mutual respect for each other. Respect is rarely given in the world. Nevertheless, it is something that must be freely given in marriage.

The scripture above notes that little foxes can get into good vines and destroy the fruit. Well, in that same sense, rudeness becomes the little fox that can creep in and hinder fruitfulness in marriage.

In all fairness, you can be rude and not know it. Look at these scenarios where rudeness shows up:

**Scenario 1**

Tonya was in her room watching television. Her husband Ben came in and lay on the bed next to her. Tonya left the room for a moment, and Ben decided to flip through the channels with the remote control. Tonya returned to discover him watching something else. When she asked him to turn back, he replied that he didn't want to view her program anymore.

Right then Tonya let Ben know he was rude. He deflected

the accusation by justifying his actions with this comment, "You've been watching what you want to watch all day, now let me watch what I want to watch." Can you see that Ben's actions were rude? The right way to handle this situation was for him to ask his wife if he could change the channel.

**Scenario 2**

Clark calls his wife at her job. He wants to know how her day is going. As they begin updating one another on the day's events, he hears his wife talking with her co-workers. Clark asks his wife if he has her attention, and she assures him that he does. As Clark continues to speak, again, he notices his wife whispering to co-workers. By now, Clark is upset and tells her that she is being rude. She defends herself by saying, "You did call me at work."

This was rude. Even though Clark called her at work, she should have asked to put him on hold, or if she could call him back, momentarily.

**Scenario 3**

When Lisa asks Paul about bill payments and banking statements he answers her in a loud abrasive tone and often makes laconic remarks. She doesn't understand his rudeness. Lisa tells him that as his wife she has the right to ask these questions. She asks why all the defensiveness. Paul dismisses her claim and says she is overly sensitive.

Paul is wrong. There is never any reason for us to holler abrasively. I know at times we get frustrated and feel the need to raise our voices, but this shows our immaturity. If this happens, and it's pointed out, quickly apologize and continue the conversation.

These were just a few examples of little foxes. However, if unchecked, little foxes often need major actions to fix them.

Sometimes couples find themselves in marital counseling or even at the verge of divorce trying to mend the messes that being rude caused.

If your marriage has been made a little messy through acts of rudeness there is a way to clean it up.

## The Cleaner

> He will be like a purifying fire and like laundry soap.
>
> —Malachi 3:2, ncv

Across America millions of wives use Woolite detergent to clean their soiled laundry. Well, good news! There is a cleaning substance for messy marriages. This cleaner is not called Woolite—it's called polite.

Love is polite! Love causes you to ask before you do. In other words, you are considerate.

In case you missed it, the common thread in all of our scenarios was no respect or consideration for the other person's feelings. To be polite, one must only consider the Golden Rule.

> Don't pick on people, jump on their failures, criticize their faults— unless, of course, you want the same treatment. That critical spirit has a way of boomeranging.
>
> —Matthew 7:1, the message

When love is assimilated in marriage, each spouse is free to be who God has called them to be. And, politeness becomes contagious. When you are polite to your spouse, they will be polite to you.

Showing politeness means that you are not taking each other

for granted, and that you appreciate your spouse in the utmost way.

Look at the following ways to exemplify politeness and care:

- Saying thank you
- Asking what your spouse thinks
- Indicating concern for your spouse's feelings
- Placing your spouse's needs ahead of yours
- Respecting your spouse's views

All of us can stand a little character enhancement. Do not permit the road block of rudeness to hold your marriage back. When you allow love to shape your character, the results are most rewarding.

# seven

# MAY I HELP YOU, PLEASE?

*Love Is Not Selfish*
*1 Corinthians 13:5*

I T IS SO IMPORTANT for couples to comprehend love in order to keep their marriage vigorous. Throughout this book we will constantly examine as well as explore the love of God.

That Christ may dwell in your hearts by faith; that ye, being rooted and grounded in love, May be able to comprehend with all saints what is the breadth, and length, and depth, and height; And to know the love of Christ, which passeth knowledge, that ye might be filled with all the fullness of God.

—EPHESIANS 3:17–19, KJV

After reading the previous scripture you should draw the conclusion that there's no getting around the love of God. The scripture speaks of understanding the breadth, length, depth and height of God's love. Of course, if you've been walking with God for any amount of time, you know that to fully exhaust God's love is impossible.

God's love denotes the quality of love that couples should express to each other. The depth, length and height of our love for our spouse should be endless. Unfortunately, this is not always the case. Normally, love expressed through human nature has boundaries. These boundaries are boxed in through selfishness.

Here is something to consider: the opposite of love is not hate. The opposite of love is selfishness.

Selfishness without a doubt stifles the growth experience of a marriage. You mark it down, every marriage, without exception, that ended in divorce was rooted in selfishness.

In 1 Corinthians 13, we come to understand the love that God abundantly gives His people. However, the very antithesis of God's love is not hate, it is selfishness.

For the most part, couples understand not to hate each other. The devil knows that placing hate in your heart is far too obvious. Therefore, his plan is for you to be consumed with self-centeredness. This selfishness takes root in your heart and the expectancy for your spouse to perform and please you becomes greater. Selfishness is a sign of immaturity, and the nature of a child is selfishness.

Many children never think about others, only what's in it for them.

> When I was a child, I spake as a child, I understood as a child, I thought as a child: but when I became a man, I put away childish things.
> —1 CORINTHIANS 13:11, KJV

The previous scripture delineates for us the three major ways that selfishness is developed in a person and manifested in a marriage. Selfishness develops through what a person speaks, what they understand and how they think. The sure fire way to dispel selfishness is by asking yourself is what I'm doing, saying or thinking glorifying God. If the answer is no then don't do it.

## SPEAK RIGHT—LOOK WHO'S TALKING

> But when they deliver you up, take no thought how or what ye shall speak: for it shall be given you in that same hour what ye shall speak. For it is not ye that speak, but the Spirit of your Father which speaketh in you.
>
> —MATTHEW 10:19–20, KJV

When we verbally communicate with our spouse in everyday life it is easy to get caught up with what is happening. Whether the issues are our children, paying the bills or even just the daily grind of running a house, married couples need to be cognizant of the words they speak to one another.

Jesus said that we can have the Holy Ghost's help when it comes to what we say. Marriages are built up or torn down based upon the very words a married couple speaks to one another. Having this knowledge, it is paramount that couples maintain a prayer life. Prayer will enable them to receive the ministry of the Holy Ghost and speak what He directs them to speak.

As couples live together and communicate with each other, there are plenty of opportunities to say the wrong thing or say the right thing the wrong way. It is during these times the Holy Ghost will give direction on what to say and how it should be said.

I can recall sharing with my wife a most unfortunate account. A couple, that she and I knew, was experiencing a case of infidelity in their marriage. I said to Andrea, "This happens when couples don't commit themselves to a life of prayer and depend on the Holy Ghost's help to keep them." I explained to her that she had to depend on the Holy Ghost's help for our marriage, too.

As I walked away the Spirit of God convicted me and said I didn't say that right. As I went back to Andrea and asked her how she took what I just said, she conveyed that she thought I was threatening infidelity if she didn't pray for the Holy Ghost's help.

Clearly, this was not the message I was trying to send. Without the Holy Ghost, I would not have sensed something wrong, nor would I have been able to clarify my point. In a marriage both people must depend upon the Holy Ghost and be willing to listen and adhere to His instructions.

It's God's Spirit that navigates us out of our selfish attitudes and into the love of God the Father.

> "Now go! I will help you speak, and will teach you what to say."
>
> —EXODUS 4:12, NCV

We are born and raised in sin. Consequently, it is God who must take and break us out of our old habits, while training us how to act and speak. The ways of the world are to be selfish. As a matter of fact, one of the world's clichés is, "Get all you can, can all you get, sit on the top, and let the rest rot." This mind-set and motto stems from the very heart of selfishness. However, in marriage, love is important and selfishness has no place. When you are married your conversation should be about how you desire your marriage and even more so, your spouse to grow. Subsequently, if all you can muster up when you speak is how you want, how you need and what's in it for you, there is something definitely wrong.

You need to stop and look who's talking!

When the Spirit talks in and through you it is usually for the benefit of someone else. Therefore, if what you're saying to your spouse is from a seed of selfishness, that didn't come from God.

Speak what God would have you say, and your marriage will continue to thrive.

Consider the case with God's servant Job. When Job was afflicted and his body covered with sores and scabs, his wife was very disparaging. She spoke out of selfishness. Perhaps, growing weary of her husband illness and hearing him cry in pain, she said curse God and even worse, she told her husband to die.

Fortunately, Job was able to look at who was talking. He identified that his wife didn't speak with the Spirit of God. Job responded by saying, "You speak like a foolish woman speaks..." Mark it down, when you are selfish, you end up sounding and coming off foolish.

Even Jesus had to endure someone speaking in an immature manner. Peter (one of the closest disciples of Jesus) rebuked our Lord, telling Him not to complete God's plan on Calvary. Jesus looked at Peter and said "Get behind me Satan..." (Matt. 16:21–23). Although Peter was the one talking, Jesus recognized that Peter's speech had been influenced by the devil.

Bottom line, when you are either talking to your spouse or listening to your spouse, especially in negative confrontation, you must look who's talking. If you detect that the message is not from God, you don't have to receive it.

## See Right—Knowing Is Half the Battle

The second way selfishness is seen through us according to 1 Corinthians 13:11 is by way of our understanding. Our understanding reflects what we have been taught.

> That the God of our Lord Jesus Christ, the Father of glory, may give unto you the spirit of wisdom and revelation in the knowledge of him: The eyes of your

understanding being enlightened; that ye may know
what is the hope of his calling, and what the riches
of the glory of his inheritance in the saints.

—EPHESIANS 1:17–18, KJV

In the same way, you husbands should live with
your wives in an understanding way, since they are
weaker than you.

—1 PETER 3:7, NCV

One of the biggest hindrances in marriage is the lack of
understanding between the husband and wife. In our society
we are taught that males and females are different. As this is a
biological fact, many of the differences are presented to us by
way of gender expectations.

Gender plays a major role in how men and women understand each other. Therefore, when these gender expectations
are not validated through either the husband or wife it could
spell trouble in the relationship. For instance, most men have
been taught that they are to be the primary breadwinner in the
marriage and if this is not the case the husband could be viewed
as a failure. This view was okay when our country was living in
the industrial age; a time when most men worked in the factory
and the women stayed home to raise the children.

Our country has since undergone some major shifts and we
are no longer in the industrial age. For that reason, both men
and women are actively working outside the home to provide
income for the family. The goal is to provide the best estate for
the family and who brings home the highest income should
not matter because both incomes are contributing to the same
cause (the couple's household).

If the couple does not have a mature understanding of this,
they will fight over whether or not the person with the highest

income should have the greater voice and decision-making power.

To be safe, let's stay where God says we should. God placed the man ahead of the woman to distinguish priority not equality. Meaning, too many husbands think the Word of God states that men are better than women. This kind of thinking couldn't be farther from the truth. God, who is the ultimate authority, knows that for any organization to work there must be structure. Every family is an organization as well. Therefore, God placed man ahead of his company (family) and the woman as his assistant.

It is safe for men to remember that Jesus is "The" Head, and the husband is ahead. If we keep that in mind men won't get a "big" head.

> But I want you to understand this: The head of every
> man is Christ, the head of a woman is the man, and
> the head of Christ is God.
> —1 CORINTHIANS 11:3, NCV

This scripture describes for us the structure of the family and how we ought to be under authority. However, this scripture only gives credence to domestic authority not civil or spiritual authority. For instance, a woman could outrank her husband in a company like the military. While at work she has authority over him, once at home she must submit to him having authority over her.

When a person is not mature they struggle with this very real principle. Thus, there is trouble in paradise and the couple begins to fight.

Women submitting regardless of their incomes has been my current example. Albeit, husbands must also understand that if the wife brings home a greater pay it doesn't make him less than her.

These gender expectations aren't relegated only to the couple's finances, but can also affect how couples relate to one another emotionally.

As it relates to emotions, it has been overstated in the past and expressed to a fault that it's okay for a woman to express her emotions, but viewed almost taboo if a man expresses his. Consequently, many marriage relationships have suffered because men pictured themselves the strong silent type. Therefore, when they needed to address certain issues in the marriage, they did not. Wives remained perplexed and husbands held captive with pent-up emotions that were never expressed.

It is absolutely selfish not to share what you are thinking or feeling with your spouse. Love compels us to express to each other what we think and feel in order that our marriage may continue to grow.

If we are to have healthy relationships we must take careful inventory of what we understand about our spouse. Our understanding should be based solely on what we have learned about our spouse as an individual. Don't rely on some antiquated pattern of gender expectations.

If not careful you can interpret understanding and thinking to be one and the same. The difference between the two is to understand begins with a thought. However, you can think without understanding being a part of the process.

I could think about whether I want to see a movie with my spouse without a full understanding of the movie. On the other hand, I must think about how spending quality time with Andrea is essential to my marriage, and having that understanding compels me to attend a movie even if I don't particularly care for the movie.

What you understand becomes a part of you and moves to

your heart, but what you think stays in your head. God wants us to lean on His understanding, not our own.

Consider the following passages.

> Consider what I say; and the Lord give thee under-standing in all things.
>
> —2 Timothy 2:7, kjv

> Behold, I have done according to thy words: lo, I have given thee a wise and an understanding heart.
>
> —1 Kings 3:12, kjv

In order for you to understand your spouse you will need to make a real effort in getting to know them. When you know your spouse, you know the unique things about their character and temperament.

There used to be a show on television called the *Newlywed Game*. This game would ask new couples specific questions about their spouse and the couple who knew the most about their spouse would win.

There are certain attributes that we must know about our spouse:

- What makes them laugh
- What makes them cry
- What their strengths are
- What their weaknesses are
- What their hopes, dreams, and goals are
- What they like
- What they dislike
- What their values are

The aforementioned enhances your ability to attend to your spouse's needs, and is paramount to maintaining a healthy marital union.

## SENSE RIGHT—YOU HAD BETTER THINK

When you get married one thing must be sure. You must be satisfied! Selfishness is diminished through satisfaction. Non-satisfaction becomes the most singular struggle that couples will face in marriage because non-satisfaction gives birth to selfishness.

What you think about your spouse is so important because it dictates how you respond to them. If you think well of your spouse, you will be determined to do well by them. Coincidently, if you do not think well about your spouse or your marriage, you will not be motivated to do well.

Paul the Apostle of Scriptures, thought enough about how we ought to think that he wrote about it on several occasions. Take a look at the next couple of passages.

> Do not be shaped by this world; instead be changed within by a new way of thinking. Then you will be able to decide what God wants for you; you will know what is good and pleasing to him and what is perfect.
>
> —ROMANS 12:2, NCV

> Does your life in Christ give you strength? Does his love comfort you? Do we share together in the spirit? Do you have mercy and kindness? If so, make me very happy by having the *same thoughts*, sharing the *same love*, and having *one mind* and purpose. When you do things, *do not let selfishness* or pride

be your guide. Instead, be humble and give more honor to others than to yourselves. Do not be interested only in your own life, but be interested in the lives of others.
—PHILIPPIANS 2:1–4, NCV, EMPHASIS ADDED

The scriptures recorded above in the book of Philippians shoot right at the very heart of this chapter. Love is not selfish! How many of us can honestly say that when we decided to get married it was on the basis of how we can add to our spouse and not the other way around?

I'm no paragon of sacrifice, but I can honestly say that when I met my wife, she already had our two sons, Omarr and Vaughn. The major factor that guided me into our marriage was the fact that I loved those boys, and knew they needed a father in their lives.

Now, don't get me wrong. I loved Andrea very much, and felt that she and I were very compatible. Notwithstanding, my decision to be there for those boys was one of the best decisions I have ever made. Thirteen years later, Andrea and I have two beautiful daughters, Jada and Ty, as well. Now we are the proud parents of four great children with a marriage union and friendship that grows stronger, each day. This was made possible because when I met Andrea I didn't think selfishly.

I have heard many say I would never marry a person who already has children. This is spoken out of a heart of selfishness. A person who has children from previous relationships doesn't automatically mean they are less of a person; it just means it's more of the person to love.

A friend of mine just recently confessed something to me that I had never heard from him before. He told me that he used to think of a woman with children as a major problem, more trouble than he cared to handle. Then he confessed that after closely monitoring my marriage and family through the years, he has a change of heart. What he once saw as a stressful situation, he now views as attractive.

I'm glad that without knowing it, Andrea and I, if only slightly, have been able to model God's love through our marriage. My friend was able to change his mind which resulted in a change of heart about marrying someone with children.

When you think with maturity and not through selfish ambitions, the results can have lasting positive effects on others around you.

## Working Against the Process of Selfishness

Let us revisit the scripture that is the outline for this chapter.

> When I was a child, I spake as a child, I understood as a child, I thought as a child: but when I became a man, I put away childish things.
> —1 Corinthians 13:11, kjv

Throughout this chapter, the thought that love is not selfish has been conveyed. Therefore, in order to have a rewarding marriage selfishness must be avoided at all cost. Through 1 Corinthians 13:11, Paul the Apostle has chronicled the process in which selfishness is displayed. Let's not miss them.

1. Speak
2. Understand
3. Think

Paul opens the scripture with, "When I was a child..." No matter how you cut it, being a child is synonymous with being selfish. Children are naturally selfish. They don't have to be taught selfishness, but rather generosity and thinking of others above themselves.

Then, Paul continues, he spoke, understood and thought like a child. Interestingly, Paul further exclaims, "When I became a man..." This becoming a man signifies his maturity.

Those who are mature are willing and often make sacrifices. These sacrifices stem from a heart of love. The classic Biblical example is found in John 3:16, "God loved the world so much that he gave his one and only Son so that whoever believed in him may not be lost, but have eternal life." Again, when Paul declared that he became a man it was a declaration of maturity. To this degree Paul finalized the scripture by stating that he put away childish things.

The question becomes, what childish things did Paul have to put away? To obtain the answer to this conundrum one need not look far. What Paul put away in maturity is what he pulled out through childishness which revealed selfishness.

Again, the process of selfishness and childishness as revealed by Paul is when we speak, understand, and then think. Therefore to avoid the process of childishness one must apply the process of maturity. The process of maturity is to simply reverse the process of childishness.

With the process of maturity first you think. Second, you understand. Last, you speak. How many problems and fights in marriage could have been avoided if both spouses employed the art of thinking before speaking?

| The Process of Childishness | The Process of Maturity |
| --- | --- |
| 1. Speak | 1. Think |
| 2. Understand | 2. Understand |
| 3. Think | 3. Speak |

Marriage is the perfect place to develop. In marriage you learn to become other people minded. Whatever you do don't waste the opportunity to distribute love to your family while developing and growing into the person God desires in the process. Remember! Love is not selfish, so continue to give and the love that you give shall be reciprocated with a hundredfold return.

# eight

# NOBODY'S PERFECT

*Love Does Not Get Upset with Others*

*1 Corinthians 13:5*

MOUNTAINTOP EXPERIENCES ARE WHAT we all strive to reach. We would all love to be at our best in any given situation. Unfortunately, this is not always the case.

There will inevitably come times in your marriage where you will see your spouse at their lowest points. It's in these times that your spouse will need you the most.

Think with me for a moment, have you ever used the phrase "Nobody's perfect"? If you have, more than likely you have used it in reference to yourself as a measure to defend some error you have made. The phrase "Nobody's perfect" is a true statement, but should not be used only for yourself, it should be extended to your spouse as well.

When love is being released in marriage it takes the short-comings that spouses have and packs them neatly away. With love you will not take your spouse's error and rub their nose in it. Love is ready to grant another chance to get it right.

> Be kind and loving to each other, and forgive each other just as God forgave you in Christ.
> —EPHESIANS 4:32, NCV

This chapter is dedicated to bringing calmness back to the marital union. I'm sure there was a time in your marriage when everything was not taken so seriously. Maybe you can recall when blunders were laughed at, and an oversight was not the end of the world. If your marriage has gotten away from those epochs, it's time to love again.

When you love your spouse, being upset is not an option. Because that can be emotionally draining, the longer you remain upset the more damage is done to your physical body and your emotions. Living in an upset state can cause stress and eventually wear you out.

Now, please do not misinterpret what I am saying. There are times when your spouse will do or say certain things that will cause anger to arise within you. If your spouse causes you to get angry at times, that's okay. Just make sure you do not hold anger in, but rather express that anger in a constructive way.

The Bible says:

> Go ahead and be angry. You do well to be angry—
> but don't use your anger as fuel for revenge. And
> don't stay angry. Don't go to bed angry. Don't give
> the Devil that kind of foothold in your life.
> —EPHESIANS 4:26–27, THE MESSAGE

We can see clearly from the previous scripture that anger is permitted as long as you don't stay in that state. Keep in mind, the Scripture also warns that a quick temper can cause trouble for us.

> People with quick tempers will have to pay for it.
> If you help them out once, you will have to do it
> again.
> —PROVERBS 19:19, NCV

> An angry person causes trouble; a person with a
> quick temper sins a lot.
> —PROVERBS 29:22, NCV

To further illuminate my point about controlling your temper, let us look at the following excerpt:

> Apply what Martin Luther used to say to negative thoughts: "You can't keep birds from flying over your head...but you can keep them from building a nest in your hair!" We may not be able to keep anger from cropping up, but we can make a decision to keep it from staying in our lives and poisoning our attitudes.[1]
> —GARY SMALLEY AND JOHN TRENT

The term *upset* does not only carry the meaning of an emotional disturbance; upset (in the way that I'm using it) means to play the role of the opposition.

Consider how the *Readers Digest Oxford Complete Wordfinder Dictionary* defines *upset*:

> *Upset*—overturn or be overturned; overcome or defeat.

The word *upset* denotes a person who is trying to defeat another in sports, if one team is up on the score the other team continues to play attempting to pull an upset. I guess now you can imagine why you should not get upset with your spouse; you are both on the same team.

There is a plethora of ways that your spouse can upset you. This chapter will cover three of these areas: mistakes, misunderstandings or misfortunes.

## Mistakes—The Common Denominator of Humanity

> Don't judge others, or you will be judged. You will
> be judged in the same way that you judge others,
> and the amount you give to others will be given to
> you. Why do you notice the little piece of dust in
> your friend's eye, but you don't notice the big piece
> of wood in your own eye? How can you say to your
> friend, "Let me take that little piece of dust out of
> your eye"? Look at yourself! You still have that big
> piece of wood in your own eye. You hypocrite! First,
> take the wood out of your own eye. Then you will
> see clearly to take the dust out of your friend's eye.
> —Matthew 7:1–5, NCV

A fraction is any mathematical quantity expressed in terms of a numerator and denominator. Some fractions have common denominators. Let's use two fractions, two-eighths and six-eighths; the common denominator is eight. Humans also have common denominators—mistakes. No one is excluded from making mistakes.

A mistake is something that cannot be avoided. Lord knows I have made my share of them. I would love to say, now that I am older I am wiser and mistakes for me are a thing of my past. Let's be real! You and I both know that it does not work that way. Mistakes come without warning. Like an unwanted guest, mistakes show up at your doorstep and you can only pray they don't stay too long.

When I think of mistakes, the account of the Prodigal Son comes to mind. Here a son demands that his father relinquishes his assets to him, and the loving father grants his son's request.

The young man goes and squanders all that his father had given him on riotous living. At his lowest point, when all of his money is spent, the son looks for his friends, and discovers like his prosperity, they have left. Although the young man had no more self-dignity, he was not out of options.

The Bible says the young man realized what an awful mistake he had made in leaving his father. Therefore, he went home with a bruised ego, a fractured heart, broke, busted and disgusted, but most importantly, he went home.

When he arrived, his father was not upset about the choices he had made. But, he found his father rejoicing and abundantly bestowing love upon him.

Can you say that you would have responded like the father? When your spouse makes mistakes do you pounce on them with an "I told you so" or do you embrace them with the words, "I love you, now let's move on."

Authentic love is not found when your spouse is on top of their game. True love is found when they not only break the rules, they do something that breaks your heart. Whether their mistakes are massive or miniscule, love can cover them all.

I have two admonishments to those who make mistakes. First, admit that you made the mistake. People often struggle with admitting that they are in error. Why hide the fact that you made a mistake? To admit it is to state that you're not perfect.

Second, stop repeating the same mistake. Mistakes can become valuable tools, but only if we learn from them. I remember hearing someone say, "If you are not going to learn from your mistakes, then don't bother making them." If you make a mistake and admit you've made the mistake, but continue in it, it's no longer a mistake, that's intentional. So, remember when you make a mistake, admit you made it, and stop making the same mistake.

In marriage there will definitely be mistakes. Either you or your spouse will do something that is not correct. When these things occur, it is certainly okay to let your spouse know about your disappointment. However, don't be too hard because the mercy you show your spouse today will be the same mercy you'll need from your spouse tomorrow.

## Misunderstanding—What You Don't Know Could Hurt

> Our marriage used to suffer from arguments that were too short. Now, we argue long enough to find out what the argument is about.[2]
>
> —Hugh Prather

Misunderstanding in marriage can be a real joy killer. If not careful, a misunderstanding can start with you both having separate opinions and end with you sleeping in separate beds.

Andrea and I have had our fair share of misunderstandings. She may feel a certain way about one thing and I may be just as adamant about my feelings toward the same thing, but I see it another way. This is natural. After all, when I met my wife one of the things that attracted me to her was her viewpoint on the matters of life.

I believe that couples spend far too much time arguing about issues that do not directly affect their marriage. On the other hand, there are times when the subject matter does directly affect it. Things like how one handles the money and budget of the family or if a spouse should have friends of the opposite sex and if so to what extent.

Is it right for your spouse to have a friend of the opposite sex? Now, here is a subject that is often misunderstood in marriage. In order to answer a question like this adequately, we must properly define the term *friend*. Let's look at two definitions of the term:

1. A person with whom one enjoys mutual affection and regard.
2. A sympathizer, helper, or patron.

Considering these two definitions, I say yes, it is okay to have a friend of the opposite sex. However, make sure that the friend falls in the second category.

Jesus is a friend to sinners and this is both male and female. In this way, we too can be friends to those of the opposite sex. Nevertheless, if your spouse is not comfortable with you having a friend of the opposite sex and even more with your choice of friend, don't push the issue. Not to mention, if you have a friend of the opposite sex they should also want to be your spouse's friend.

The caveat that I would like to add to this discussion on friends with the opposite sex is—be very careful. The reason for the caution is if your spouse is not giving you the support you need, but a friend of the opposite sex is, this can lead to an illicit sexual encounter (infidelity).

What is more important is your friendship with your spouse who happens to fall in the category of the first definition. The real question becomes, do you love your spouse? Do not place others above the relationship that you have with your spouse.

Whatever you do, never allow a misunderstanding to cause you to miss what God has for your marriage, and ultimately miss the hand of God in your marriage. There are things that God desires for you and your spouse, but He cannot do them because misunderstandings have you in disagreement.

> In the same way, you husbands should live with
> your wives in an understanding way, since they are
> weaker than you. But show them respect, because
> God gives them the same blessing he gives you—the
> grace that gives true life. Do this so that nothing
> will stop your prayers.
>
> —1 PETER 3:7, NCV

In the Bible there was a man by the name of Naaman who
almost missed God because he let his misunderstanding get in
the way (2 Kings 5:1–15).

Naaman had a disease and was desperately looking for a
cure when he came to God's prophet. After receiving instructions from a servant of God's prophet, Naaman became both
angry and offended.

> Naaman lost his temper. He turned on his heel
> saying, "I thought he'd personally come out and meet
> me, call on the name of GOD, wave his hand over
> the diseased spot, and get rid of the disease…He
> stomped off, mad as a hornet.
>
> —2 KINGS 5:11, THE MESSAGE

Naaman got upset because the prophet did not respond to
the situation the way he thought the prophet should have.

His story is the direct reflection of many of our marriages.
We get upset with our spouse because we feel they did not do
something the way we felt they should have.

One morning, I got up bright and early to mow the lawn. My
intentions were to cut the grass and finish before the sun rose. I
also promised my sons that I would drive them to school.

With no time to spare, I began cutting. Everything was going
according to my plans until my wife came bursting out of the

house yelling at me to take my youngest daughter, Ty, over to someone else's house.

Now, this new mission was totally unexpected. I asked Andrea why she couldn't take Ty. Her answer was she would be late for work and that I had time to do it. Needless to say, I was upset. I, too, had to be at work and for this reason I got up extra early so I could cut the grass, get ready for work and drop my sons off at school.

That day Andrea's misunderstanding came off as complete inconsideration. I, like Naaman, felt that Andrea could have done what she did another way. However the imposition, my daughter, had to be dropped off.

Later I did express my disappointment to Andrea. She apologized and admitted that she thought I didn't have to go to work since I was cutting grass. No matter how upset I was at the time, my love for Andrea allowed me to forgive and move on.

Again, misunderstandings happen all the time in marriage. The best way to handle them is to discuss them openly with your spouse. The one thing that should never be misunderstood is the love that you have for one another. It's that love that will carry you through.

## MISFORTUNE—CARE TO BE THERE

Once you are married, I believe your primary duty is being there for your spouse. Most of us confessed within our wedding vows, "for better or for worse." When confessing this did we really intend on being there for worse?

I know of couples who had big dreams of doing things together. Suddenly one of them became very ill. Now the questions start. What do you do when you have to wash and dress another adult? What do you do when the person you stood at the altar with can no longer stand? Well, I'll tell you what these spouses did. They cared to be there.

Misfortune is another issue that we all have to face. When confronted with misfortune you can choose to get upset or you can choose to convert adversity into advantage.

The one thing we should never do is become upset with our spouse when adversity hits. This only compounds the problem. The Bible tells of a man, named Job, who had to face all sorts of misfortunes. He lost his children to death; he lost his land, his money and even his health. His wife (instead of comforting him) got upset and confronted him with this statement, "Curse God and die!"

This had to be a horrifying blow. The woman he married, the mother of his children, got upset and wished him dead. Just think! What if your spouse, like Job's wife, had the bedside manners of Scrooge?

Amazingly, Job was able to recover from his losses without the direct assistance of his wife. Job gives us an example to live by. When your spouse is adding pressure to an already volatile situation, look to God. He'll give the strength you need to pull through.

You should never have to fight a battle alone. In marriage a spouse is there to add protection, affection, and comfort. Consider the following scripture.

> It's better to have a partner than go it alone. Share
> the work, share the wealth. And if one falls down,
> the other helps, But if there's no one to help, tough!
> —ECCLESIASTES 4:9–10, THE MESSAGE

I can recall early in our marriage, Andrea and I decided that I would be responsible to pay our monthly bills. One particular month I went into the cable company to make a payment. After

I had conducted business, I went out to my car headed to my next destination.

Then I realized that I had left the envelope which had all of our money in it on the counter at the cable company. I hurried back into that building, rushed up to the counter where I had made my payment and the envelope was gone.

I frantically searched around the area. I asked the agent who had assisted me if she saw my envelope. She said a woman who had stood behind me in line took my envelope and left.

Due to laws the cable company was unable to give me any information about the woman who had taken my money. Feeling dejected and defeated I went home to face the music and my wife.

All I could think about was how upset Andrea would be, how I let my family down, and how I must appear to be an irresponsible person. Once home, I told Andrea what had happened. As I prepared myself for the worse, she looked me in the eyes noticing my obvious pain, and said, "Honey its okay, we'll make it." Although I didn't feel immediate relief, Andrea's soft spoken words eventually ameliorated my current situation. It also reminded me that "Nobody's perfect." When my wife had every right to get upset with me she chose not to. Just two words gave what was otherwise a depressing situation hope. "Nobody's perfect!"

Like sun rays breaking through a darkened sky, these words empowered me to erect from my slumped posture and to finish what I started. I paid the bills that month and for the next thirteen years of our marriage (I wasn't fired). I'm elated to say, I never missed a payment and I never lost our money again. I give God all the glory, and I truly thank my wife.

Misfortune visits everyone. During tough times is when couples need one another the most. The love you have will be the difference between misfortunes overtaking you or over-coming them.

Please remember your spouse is not perfect, and you aren't either. We are all going to make mistakes, misunderstand and have misfortunes. Applying love in all these situations will preserve your marriage and ensure unity.

# nine

# THAT'S THREE STRIKES!

*Love Does Not Count Wrongs*
*1 Corinthians 13:5*

IT HAS BEEN SUGGESTED that baseball is America's game. Although I personally know of a few people who would argue the veracity of such a statement, I find the rules that govern the game intriguing.

What I find particularly interesting in baseball is that a man while at bat must hit a ball that the pitcher is throwing. If the man misses a thrown pitch, this is called a strike. If the man has three strikes he is considered "out" and is no longer at bat.

Now if you are not an aficionado of baseball you might say, "What's so interesting about that?" Well I say, "Pressure!" It is extremely demanding to be asked to accomplish something knowing that every error is being counted against you.

Unfortunately, this kind of scorekeeping and faultfinding is not only in baseball, it has crept into the modern marriage. Couples often tally the errors that each other make. This sort of pressure is unnecessary and can take its toll on a perfectly good marriage.

A young couple was becoming anxious about their four-year-old son who had not yet talked. They took him to specialist, but the doctors found nothing wrong with him. Then one morning at breakfast the boy suddenly blurted, "Mom, the toast is burned." "You talked! You talked!" shouted the mother. "I'm so happy! But why has it taken this long?" "Well, up till now," said the boy, "things have been okay."

In like manner, some marriages have gotten so bad that the only time the couple verbally communicates is to complain about the other's shortcomings.

A good question to ask is, "How do I keep from judging my spouse?" Contemplate the following forewarning from scripture.

> Don't pick on people, jump on their failures, criticize their faults—unless, of course, you want the same treatment. That critical spirit has a way of boomeranging. It's easy to see a smudge on your neighbor's face and be oblivious to the ugly sneer on your own. Do you have the nerve to say, "Let me wash your face for you," when your own face is distorted by contempt? It's this whole traveling road-show mentality all over again, playing a holier-than-thou part instead of just living your part. Wipe that ugly sneer off your own face, and you might be fit to offer a washcloth to your neighbor.
>
> —MATTHEW 7:1–5, THE MESSAGE

The preceding scripture is pretty explicit about not judging someone else. When you count up all the wrongs that your spouse has done in order to throw them back in their face, you only display a spirit of ingratitude.

As married people, we must be aware of the power that we possess to either build our spouse up or tear them down. Author Rick Johnson tells of how women carry the ability to ignite or defuse the motivation of their husbands. He compares a woman to a horse whisperer and a man is likened to a horse.

Johnson gives a compelling difference between a horse trainer and a horse whisperer.

What is the difference between the "horse trainer" and the "horse whisperer?"...The trainer simply demands the horse comply and fit into his world. In essence the trainer creates an obedient, castrated, brow-beaten pet...The horse whisperer, however, quietly observes and listens, and notes, and then gently enters the animal's world to make contact that is full of trust, rather than fear. The horse whisperer is compassionate, wise, and tender, yet firm. The result? An animal who trust the whisperer, because the whisperer respects the animal. They form a pleasant, mutually giving relationship, and the horse and rider are both better for it.[1]

—RICK JOHNSON

The point is that both husband and wife should desire to build one another up. This can be accomplished when they learn and encourage each other.

You cannot encourage your spouse while constantly reminding them about the times they have not hit the mark. There is a three-step process I use to prevent counting my wife's wrongs.

## YOU NEVER FORGET!

For I will be merciful to their unrighteousness, and
their sins and their iniquities will I remember no
more.

—HEBREWS 8:12, KJV

This verse of scripture has always been a source of reassuring
comfort to me. Just imagine, God who knows all my frailties
and faults will never bring them up again. Even though the
Scriptures tell us that God chooses to forget our wrongs, we
still remember our wrongs.

To remember the wrongs that you have committed is vital to
your character; it should keep you humble. Some people never
forget their past and it haunts them. I am not suggesting you
should hold on to bad memories or past hurts. Whatever you
do, never allow yourself to become the walking wounded. I
mean wherever you go you are always telling someone about
your mistakes. Just remember that you have made mistakes or
have done wrong; and it won't be difficult to grant your spouse
a pass when they do wrong.

My father likes to use the term "ex"-men. He says that we
are all "ex" something. You could be an ex-thief, ex-alcoholic,
ex-adulterer; whatever it is nobody's past is squeaky clean. God
saw with "x"-ray vision our "ex" condition, and through His
love and compassion forgave and took us in as His very own.

Therefore if any man be in Christ, he is a new crea-
ture: old things are passed away; behold, all things
are become new.

—2 CORINTHIANS 5:17, KJV

Take a look at another scripture to amplify God's mercy covering our wrongs.

> I beseech you therefore, brethren, by the mercies of God, that ye present your bodies a living sacrifice, holy, acceptable unto God, which is your reasonable service.
>
> —ROMANS 12:1, KJV

If we do not forget God had to show mercy for our wrongs, we will not have a problem serving Him. I don't know about you, but when the Psalmist wrote, "The steadfast love of the Lord never ceases, His mercies and grace never ends. They are new every morning" (Lam. 3:22–24, author's paraphrase), I shouted, "Hallelujah!" I need them every morning.

## YOU MUST FORGIVE!

Throughout this book you will continue to read about forgiveness. This is largely due to the fact forgiveness plays a major role in marriage. It is something you will have to put into practice if you are going to stay married.

Therefore, if you never forget your wrongs have been forgiven; you will forgive your spouse.

An insurance agent was writing a policy for a cowboy. "Have you ever had any accidents?" the agent asked. "No, not really," replied the cowboy. "A horse kicked in a few of my ribs once. I got bit a couple of times by a rattlesnake, but that's about it." "Don't you call those accidents?" demanded the agent. "Oh, no," came the answer, "they did that on purpose."

It can be difficult to forgive your spouse at times. It's especially hard when you feel the offence was deliberate. However, it is extremely important to forgive. God commands you to forgive, and His command is based on the fact that He has forgiven you.

Consider the following scriptures:

> At that point Peter got up the nerve to ask, "Master, how many times do I forgive a brother or sister who hurts me? Seven?" Jesus replied, "Seven! Hardly. Try seventy times seven. The kingdom of God is like a king who decided to square accounts with his servants. As he got under way, one servant was brought before him who had run up a debt of a hundred thousand dollars. He couldn't pay up, so the king ordered the man, along with his wife, children, and goods, to be auctioned off at the slave market. The poor wretch threw himself at the king's feet and begged, 'Give me a chance and I'll pay it all back.' Touched by his plea, the king let him off, erasing the debt. The servant was no sooner out of the room when he came upon one of his fellow servants who owed him ten dollars. He seized him by the throat and demanded, 'Pay up. Now!' The poor wretch threw himself down and begged, 'Give me a chance and I'll pay it all back.' But he wouldn't do it. He had him arrested and put in jail until the debt was paid. When the other servants saw this going on, they were outraged and brought a detailed report to the king. The king summoned the man and said, 'You evil servant! I forgave your entire debt when you begged me for mercy. Shouldn't you be compelled to be merciful to your fellow servant who asked for mercy?' The king was furious and put the screws to the man until he paid back his entire

debt. And that's exactly what my Father in heaven is going to do to each one of you who doesn't forgive unconditionally anyone who asks for mercy."

—MATTHEW 18:21–35, THE MESSAGE

As established in the preceding scriptures, God requires that we all forgive because we have all been forgiven by our King. This parable indicates God will punish us if we do not forgive others.

A pastor named Raul gave an actual account that beautifully portrays the mercy and forgiveness of God. The pastor says that as a child he and his siblings shared a mutt who they named Fleas. The only food that they would give their dog was the leftovers from each meal. The dog especially liked bones and would immediately bury them for later consumption.

One day after Fleas buried his biggest bone, Raul being mischievous, went out, dug up Fleas' bone and reburied it someplace else. Later, when Fleas returned, Raul watched and laughed as Fleas dug frantically for the missing bone. He said Fleas dug himself almost to China and still no bone.

Years later as an adult, Pastor Raul committed multiple sins. While he was feeling regret and despair for his sins, God spoke to him and said, "Just as you hid Fleas' bone many years ago, that is what I have done for you. Your sins, like his bones, have been removed. They are no longer where you left them."

When it comes to our sins, God is the Bone Collector. He takes those skeletons from our closets and places them where we don't have to see them. Like Raul's dog, Fleas, you can dig until you reach China, and the only thing you'll find is God's forgiveness.

Since God has forgiven you, be ready to forgive others (especially your spouse).

## YOU WILL FORGET!

I have heard people say after being hurt, "I'll forgive, but I won't forget." I submit unto you, when you truly forgive, you will forget.

Now, I'm not implying that a person should suppress negative emotions; nor should you deny that something bad has happened by burying it in the subconscious. However, you can forgive and forget.

My wife and I have had arguments in the past where negative and hurtful things were spoken. We have apologized and to this day neither one of us can remember what was said.

When you love someone the last thing you want to do is think of them in a negative way or hold them in a bad light. Love will allow you to forget the negatives and focus on the positives.

Your marriage becomes like a picture taken with a disposable camera. The photograph is developed in the dark room, and when you receive your picture it is accompanied with a negative. Nobody frames or looks at the negatives but they're there.

When you look at your spouse you want their picture in your heart. You don't need to stare at the negatives. Put them away. When bad things happen in marriage or the wrongs things are said, cheer up, you're being developed in the dark room of life.

Take a look at what pastor and author Jack W. Hayford says, on the subject of forgiving:

> True forgiveness springs from gratitude to God for His forgiving me. True forgiveness is born of my remembrance that I have been forgiven so great a debt through God's love, there is no justification for my being less than fully forgiving to others. Because

I have "freely received," my Lord calls me to "freely give." To forgive those seeking to injure you or me is to remove ourselves from their control and to be unfettered by the anger, pain, or disappointment that would seek to attach itself to us.[2]

Friend, when you forget what your spouse has done you are not being manipulated or controlled. That's the power of forgiveness!

What happens when you truly forgive your spouse but a thought continues to play back in your mind? Well, you just simply say, I forgive them again. This is what Jesus was telling Peter when He said to forgive seventy times seven. Whenever necessary, forgive again, and again, and again. Eventually the time will come when you will no longer need to forgive because you will no longer remember the offence.

Love doesn't sit around counting the wrongs your spouse has done. Love helps you to remember and cherish all the right things they have added to your life.

If you've been at bat in marriage and struck out, don't give up, there are more innings left.

*ten*

# THE DANGER of CHEATING

*Love Is Not Happy with Evil*
*1 Corinthians 13:6*

A S PERFECT AS WE would like marriage to be, as sacred as it should be kept, some marriages have undergone the gross betrayal of infidelity.

One of the pillars of marriage is trust. Without trust a happy and productive marriage is impossible. Spouses depend and look to each other to be trustworthy.

A covenant marriage is not viewed as an experience but more importantly, a commitment, an obligation lived out.

God established marriage to show His love for humanity. You've probably seen some pretty bad marriages in your day. So, the question becomes, "Were those marriages full of the love of God?" The obvious answer is, "Of course not!" Marriage was never intended to make us perfect; but to show we can be loved with imperfections. This is God's love, a love that never ends.

Marriage provides discipline. As Christians, we aspire to be disciplined in every area of our lives. Jesus taught the first disciples to be disciplined. Starting in their prayer life, Jesus did not tell them to pray any way. He said, "When ye pray, say..." (Luke 11:1–4, KJV).

God commands us to love and worship Him only. However, there are those who have a god for everything. In Greek mythology they worshiped the god of the sun, another god of the water, another god of nature and so on. This kind of divided loyalty can be carried into our relationships. If you can't serve the One True God, chances are you will have trouble serving just one husband or wife.

Allow me to use this illustration:

When dining out, you can choose an exquisite restaurant or an all-you-can-eat buffet. The exquisite restaurant has a menu from which you select a meal. However, the buffet has food that everyone picks through.

People who are not married but have decided to remain single (just dating) reveal a "buffet mentality." They have to partake of what others are picking through. Those who are married should enjoy the person they have selected from God's menu. This exquisite person is prepared just for them.

A lack of discipline in marriage can present the danger of committing adultery.

## WHY DO PEOPLE CHEAT?

I have sat in many counseling sessions listening to the heart-ache of an individual as they try reasoning why their spouse has cheated.

Although there are many reasons a person might forfeit their "Covenant," I wish to share three.

- Lack of character—when a person is missing fundamental qualities like loyalty, trustwor-thiness, and honor they will have no problem committing adultery.
- Low self-esteem—a person who does not feel good about themself will always need someone else to lift their spirit or boost their ego.
- Little self-control—this person yields to their lusts and displays no self-discipline.

Some people have a phobia about marriage. They are convinced that when it comes to marriage, it's not a question of *will* their spouse cheat, but rather *when* their spouse will cheat on them.

Then there are those who have had to undergo this horrible act. Their concern is not only *will*, or *when*, but *where*. This person watches their spouse's every move, constantly thinking; will this be the next person, will this be the next place.

Do not allow your mind to become a haunted house troubled with ghosts of the past, present or future. In other words, you won't concern yourself with the *will*, *when* or *where* of cheating if you understand *why*.

When you know why a person commits adultery you can defeat the devil on his turf. Whether married or single you can look at these three reasons and deal with them accordingly.

It really helps to know and have a relationship with God when you are married. If you ask, God will impart his Spirit into you whereby empowering you to overcome the obstacle of cheating.

The Bible teaches us that Samson had God's help. However, he did not reverence his Nazarite vows. Samson broke his covenant, but before we scrutinize his indiscretions we need to learn from him.

Early in his life, the power of God's Spirit was not Samson's focus. He was distracted by the women of the world. We can be distracted, too. Without God's Spirit influencing us we can find ourselves entangled in the yoke of cheating.

If we are not careful we can set our affections on stature, statutes, and status by neglecting the presence of God's Spirit.

Stature: Going after growth, development, and achievement
Statute: Obeying government laws, rules, and regulations
Status: Position and rank in relation to others

The devil is always in opposition to the plan of God, and constantly attacking marriages. He only needs the answer to one question in order to destroy your marriage, "Are you for sale?"

## Not for Sale!

The president of a company walked over to one of his female employee's desk and boldly asked the woman, "Will you sleep with me for one hundred thousand dollars?" The woman, totally caught off guard, with a slight grin, responded, "Well, yes, I think I would." "Will you sleep with me for fifty thousand dollars?" the president enquired. The woman still quite shocked responded, "I'm sorry you came down from your original amount, but yes. I would sleep with you for fifty thousand." Then the president moved in closer to the woman and whispered, "How about fifty dollars? Will you sleep with me for fifty dollars?" The woman now offended by the employer's drastic deduction in number said, "What kind of woman do you think I am?" The president quickly replied, "We've already established what kind of woman you are, now, we're just negotiating a price."

My friend, this is the exact ploy of the devil. He will come and tempt you with something that seems nice, but the end result is always devastating. It might be that co-worker who always compliments the way you dress, smell or speak. You may find yourself thinking, I wish my spouse said these things to me, or I wish my spouse was that smart. Do not become misled. The devil wants to know if you are for sale.

> Let no man say when he is tempted, I am tempted of God: for God cannot be tempted with evil, neither tempteth he any man: But every man is tempted,

when he is drawn away of his own lust, and enticed.
Then when lust hath conceived, it bringeth forth sin:
and sin, when it is finished, bringeth forth death.

—James 1:13–15, KJV

The notion of being for sale means you can be tempted with evil. Mark it down; anyone who can be tempted with evil does not have the Spirit of God operating in their life. When the Spirit of God is alive within, you are protected from every trap the devil sets.

The aforementioned scripture says that every man is tempted when he is drawn away by his own lust. Therefore, the key is not to lust after things or people. When you become married you must replace the "for sale" with "sold out." Again, the married life is a representation of Christ's love for His people. So, you must be sold out to God first, then to your spouse.

If you're living an adulterous life, don't give up hope. Like Hosea pursued Gomer, God is pursuing you. If God is willing to go after you, just receive His love.

> Then God ordered me, "Start all over: Love your wife again, your wife who's in bed with her latest boyfriend, your cheating wife. Love her the way I, God, love the Israelite people, even as they flirt and party with every god that takes their fancy." I did it. I paid good money to get her back. It cost me the price of a slave. Then I told her, "From now on you're living with me. No more whoring, no more sleeping around. You're living with me and I'm living with you."
>
> —Hosea 3:1–3, The Message

Many people cheat on their spouse for a myriad of reasons. The devastating results are: you dishonor God, you destroy the trust of your family, and you jeopardize everything you have built.

The danger of cheating is that you have broken your covenant. Make no mistake about it; there are consequences when a covenant is broken.

## The Consequences in Breaking Covenant

> But the Philistines took him, and put out his eyes, and brought him down to Gaza, and bound him with fetters of brass; and he did grind in the prison house.
>
> —Judges 16:21, kjv

From conception Samson was dedicated to live a life set apart for God. In other words, he was to be God's covenant man. His parents raised him to respect and honor God's commands. And, as long as Samson lived according to God's rules, God moved mightily on his behalf.

Unfortunately, as Samson grew in stature he diminished spiritually. He had no real reverence for God or His covenant. Samson began breaking the covenant stipulations one by one. As a result, he became blind, bound and carried a heavy burden. The tactics the enemy used to destroy Samson are the same tactics he uses to destroy us when we break covenant.

### Blind

> But the Philistines took him, and put out his eyes.
>
> —Judges 16:21

Blindness is the first destroyer that manifests when you cheat. You are no longer able to see what is important and of value. Your spouse, the apple of your eye, has been tossed aside for forbidden fruit. Your lust has led to another address. Your covetousness has caused callousness. Although you share a house, you no longer share hearts.

Adultery is that armed robber who takes your innocence. Your motive should be to see your family succeed. However, cheating has a way of obscuring your family view.

No matter how you cut it, cheating does two things—*deceive* and *deprive*. Through deception others are made to believe your lie. You become someone you are not in order to live a double life. The ultimate chicanery is that you and the one you are cheating with have become liars; two liars can't trust each other. Not only that, you have defiled your sacred and pure marriage.

Likewise, your spouse is deprived of what they rightfully deserve—pure love and honest intentions. Some cheat on their spouse without trying to end their marriage. This is called an extramarital affair. They want to keep their marriage, they just want extra. Although this term might have a nice ring to it, the sting of it is quite harmful.

Let me make one point very clear, you cannot cheat and keep your marriage intact. The mere fact of cheating deprives your marriage from moving forward. Every time you are with someone else, time is stolen from your marriage. Your marriage moves when both you and your spouse are devoting time to move it. Anything deprived lacks what it needs to develop.

*Deprivation dwarfism* occurs when there's a lack of emotional attention given to children. The result leads to stunted growth. This phenomenon is discovered in some cases where some sort of abuse or lack is present. Figuratively speaking, your marriage can experience deprivation dwarfism if it is not nurtured with love and affection.

Remember, one of the devil's strategies is the lust of the eyes.

> For all that is in the world, the lust of the flesh, and the lust of the eyes, and the pride of life, is not of the Father, but is of the world.
>
> —1 JOHN 2:16, KJV

The devil wants you to look at someone with desire for one second. He knows if you'll look for one second, you'll look for a minute. Then, he'll tempt you with one hour or perhaps a day, etc. This is what he did in the Garden. He convinced Eve to desire something God said she and Adam should not have.

> And when the woman saw that the tree was good for food, and that it was pleasant to the eyes, and a tree to be desired to make one wise, she took of the fruit thereof, and did eat, and gave also unto her husband with her; and he did eat.
>
> —GENESIS 3:6, KJV

The previous verse of scripture is packed with so much revelation. At first glance, you would look at this scripture and think, what's the big deal? The tree was in fact good for food and could make her wise, is that so bad? It is when you consider what Eve did. Adam and Eve broke God's commandment.

Ultimately, Eve's actions caused her husband to do wrong. When you are blind you become myopic, you can barely see what's directly in front of you and you lose all foresight.

Because you are a cheater, your spouse can become a cheater as well. Maybe you are a one or two-time cheater, but who's to say, your spouse may become a notorious cheater. Now, be honest, are you willing to take that chance? Do like God's servant Job, make a covenant with your eyes so you don't even think about anyone else except your spouse (Job 31:1, KJV).

## Bound

> But the Philistines took him...and bound him with fetters of brass.
>
> —JUDGES 16:21, KJV

With euphemisms like *sleeping around* and *having an affair*, adultery sounds pretty festive. These are different terms that the world uses to cover up adultery. Adultery is really harsh and offensive.

These euphemisms are like a spider's web. They are used to mask the fact that adultery is cruel and harmful. Therefore, you are not able to see and detest the havoc adultery causes until it's too late (you can't see a spider's web until you are caught in it). The more you move in the web, the tighter the hold on you. Then along comes the spider to wrap you in its binding cocoon to slowly suck the life out of you.

Satan invites you into an affair with someone else. You think, "affair" does not sound bad at all. Before you realize it, this affair has you wrapped into a cocoon and you are unable to get free. Instead of thinking of cheating as an affair, see yourself as a slave to your secrets.

Becoming a "slave to your secrets" is a term my wife uses to describe those who practice a life of sin and attempt to hide it. Basically, you and Satan have a secret that he can't wait to tell. Harboring this secret (in this case adultery) causes you to become bound in your mind, resulting in a stronghold.

> For the weapons of our warfare are not carnal, but
> mighty through God to the pulling down of strong
> holds.
>
> —2 CORINTHIANS 10:4, KJV

The word *stronghold* means fortress or anything which one relies on. In the previous verse of scripture the connotation is one who argues or tries to fortify his position through reasoning against opposition. In other words, in your heart you know it's not right to cheat on your spouse, but you reason why you do. You back yourself into a corner and become bound to this position. This is a position against your spouse, and more importantly against God.

My friend, this is the plan of Satan. He will set up occasions where you can be alone with someone. He will have someone come your way that will say all the right words and do all the right things. He is looking to sever your relationship with your spouse and ultimately destroy your relationship with God.

Consider the following scripture:

> After all, we don't want to unwittingly give Satan an
> opening for yet more mischief—we're not oblivious
> to his sly ways!
>
> —2 CORINTHIANS 2:11, THE MESSAGE

Also, when you think of becoming bound, think of being restricted in movement. I mean you must give up some liberties. For instance, you might have to monitor where you leave your cell phone so your spouse doesn't become aware of certain calls. You have to be careful about your whereabouts and who sees you with your lover.

Think of your life with your spouse as a box. This may not be the best illustration; however, bear with me while I attempt to make my point. If you commit adultery you are adding someone else in the box which reduces the allotted space in your box, thus, you become bound. The more people in your box the less movement you have.

Allow me to further amplify my point by using the following scriptures:

> It will save you from the unfaithful wife who tries to lead you into adultery with pleasing words. She leaves the husband she married when she was young. She ignores the promise she made before God.
>
> —PROVERBS 2:16–17, NCV

> She threw her arms around him and kissed him, boldly took his arm and said, "I've got all the makings for a feast—today I made my offerings, my vows are all paid, So now I've come to find you, hoping to catch sight of your face—and here you are! I've spread fresh, clean sheets on my bed, colorful imported linens. My bed is aromatic with spices and exotic fragrances. Come, let's make love all night, spend the night in ecstatic lovemaking! My husband's not home; he's away on business, and he won't be back for a month." Soon she has him eating out of her hand, bewitched by her honeyed speech. Before you know it, he's trotting behind her, like a calf led to the butcher shop, Like a stag lured into ambush and then shot with an arrow, Like a bird flying into a net not knowing that its flying life is over.
>
> —PROVERBS 7:13–23, THE MESSAGE

The woman in Proverbs 2 ignores the promise (covenant) she has with God. The woman in Proverbs 7 causes her victim to become bewitched and eventually has him caught in her net. In essence, the man becomes bound. These are just a few cautionary tales the Bible gives to steer us clear of violating our covenant with our spouse and God.

**Burden**

> But the Philistines took him... and he did grind in the prison house.
>
> —JUDGES 16:21, KJV

I'm amazed how people who commit adultery and are eventually caught expect to be forgiven immediately. The guilty person apologizes to their spouse, then feels their spouse shouldn't make certain demands.

If you have committed adultery and are currently working toward reconciliation you must understand your spouse has been devastated. They need time to recover. Stating it mildly, you are going to have to put in some work.

Don't complain if your spouse asks to examine your cell phone records or requests that you abstain from constantly checking e-mails. Your spouse may feel uncomfortable when you're not home and will want you there more often. Whatever it takes to regain their confidence, just do it. Remember, you caused the damage. Trust in the relationship has been destroyed and will take work to repair.

I know of a situation where an individual cheated on their spouse. One of the steps toward recovery was the cheating partner had to undergo psychiatric treatment. Having psychiatrists probe into your mind can be a burden.

Infidelity not only places a burden on the guilty spouse, it can be an enormous weight on the entire family. In the Bible, Potiphar was the master of a young man named Joseph. God caused everything Potiphar had to prosper for Joseph's sake (Gen. 39:5). However, in Potiphar's absence, his wife made continual sexual advances toward Joseph. Yet, Joseph didn't succumb to her. Nevertheless, she lied about him and Potiphar had Joseph incarcerated. As a result Potiphar's entire estate no longer experienced the blessing of God. This adulterous act of his wife brought hardship on their entire household.

Most often, sexual indiscretions bring shame and disappointment on an entire family. Children can become affected if they are old enough to understand the offense.

Families have undergone financial burdens because of adultery. We see it every day in the news. There has been a proliferation of politicians and clergy asked to resign from their positions because of a lack of integrity. This can cause their family to lose wages. If you truly love your family, love them enough not to place this burden upon them.

Finally, the Bible teaches we are capable of passing down generational curses. When we develop bad habits they could be passed to our children. This is the sin of the fathers visiting the sons. In the world, it's stated, "The apple does not fall too far from the tree."

King David had a man killed in order to take his wife. And, his son Solomon's troubles stemmed from his dealings with women. Jacob tricked his father to get his brother's birthright; years later, his older sons tricked him about Joseph's death.

Having your children and your children's children carry your sin can be a tremendous burden.

## Broken Covenants Can Be Fixed

And Samson called unto the LORD, and said, O Lord
God, remember me, I pray thee, and strengthen me,
I pray thee.

—Judges 16:28, KJV

Realize breaking the covenant of your marriage causes blindness, binding and burdens. Fortunately, you can recover from these states. First, you must seek God's forgiveness. Second, you must seek the forgiveness of your spouse. Third, you must forgive yourself.

David committed adultery with Bathsheba and a child was conceived out of this ungodly union (2 Sam. 11:3–5). When confronted by God, David asked the Lord's forgiveness (2 Sam. 12:13).

Look at David's apologetic psalm:

God, be merciful to me because you are loving.
Because you are always ready to be merciful, wipe
out all my wrongs. Wash away all my guilt and
make me clean again.... Create in me a pure heart,
God, and make my spirit right again.... God, save
me from the guilt of murder, God of my salvation.

—Psalm 51:1–2, 10, 14, NCV

Adultery directly offends God because you and your spouse belong to Him. He takes infidelity as a personal attack, and most people don't want to fight with God. If you take this into consideration, I'm sure you won't commit such an offensive act.

After you have asked for God's forgiveness you must look to reconcile with your spouse. Don't mince words! Without circumlocution, you must ask your spouse for forgiveness. Keep in mind God forgives the minute you repent, but your spouse will need time to process the offence. There must be time allotted for healing to occur.

> So when you offer your gift to God at the altar, and you remember that your brother or sister has something against you, leave your gift there at the altar. Go and make peace with that person, and then come and offer your gift.
>
> —MATTHEW 5:23–24, NCV

The preceding scripture says if your brother or sister has something against you go and make peace with them. Your spouse is also your brother or sister in the Lord.

Keith and Michelle had a picture-book marriage. They were a young couple, madly in love with each other and the Lord. Michelle was pregnant with Keith's second child. On the day Michelle gave birth, she discovered that Keith had been committing adultery. She was devastated. In one day, she went from experiencing an all time high with the birth of their second child to an ultimate low through experiencing the consummate betrayal.

Keith, being dumbfounded, did not know what to say. He couldn't believe how he had allowed his temptation to bring such damage to his marriage and pain to his wife, his friend. Keith with much contrition asked for Michelle's forgiveness.

Michelle, obviously hurt, thought long and hard about ending the marriage. While contemplating this very real option she decided to call her close friend. Her friend consoled and instructed Michelle to seek the assistance of her pastor on the delicate matter. Michelle and Keith did just that. After receiving pastoral counseling and seeing Keith's apparent pain for causing all of this grief, Michelle decided to forgive him.

It has been months since the incident was revealed. Keith has since had to reestablish trust with Michelle. It hasn't been easy, but with love they have been working through it.

I am so proud of Michelle. She is one of God's heroes of faith because the best of us can talk about love, but when the true test comes will we put love on display?

The final step to repairing the broken covenant is forgiving yourself. If you're anything like me, sometimes you can be your worse critic.

Theologians argue after David committed adultery and was confronted with his sin, he found it hard to forgive himself. They also purport, when David's son Absalom murdered his brother Amnon, David's failure to respond could have been linked to him not forgiving his own sexual sins.

You must forgive yourself in order to go further and be effective in what God has called and commissioned you to do. There was a woman who was caught in the very act of adultery. Let's read this account from Scripture:

> The religion scholars and Pharisees led in a woman who had been caught in an act of adultery. They stood her in plain sight of everyone and said, "Teacher, this woman was caught red-handed in the act of adultery. Moses, in the Law, gives orders to stone such persons. What do you say?" They were trying to trap him into saying something incriminating so they could bring charges against him. Jesus bent down and wrote with his finger in the dirt. They kept at him, badgering him. He straightened up and said, "The sinless one among you, go first: Throw the stone." Bending down again, he wrote some more in the dirt. Hearing that, they walked away, one after

another, beginning with the oldest. The woman was left alone. Jesus stood up and spoke to her. "Woman, where are they? Does no one condemn you?" "No one, Master." "Neither do I," said Jesus. "Go on your way. From now on, don't sin."

—John 8:3–11, the message

Others wanted to see her punished. However, what we are privileged to see is God's mercy. I'm truly touched by the heart of God. Here we have a woman who was as guilty as sin. Amazingly, through the love of God she was not condemned. Likewise, neither was her sin condoned. Jesus told the woman to go and sin no more.

Now, I have heard this account told numerous times. Scholars and preachers have tried to convey what they thought Jesus wrote in the dirt. To be perfectly honest, I do not care what Jesus was scribbling with his finger. What's more profound is the mere fact that Jesus had His finger in the dirt. We serve a God who is not too good to get down in dirt where we often are.

When we have a Savior like Jesus, and wives and husbands like Michelle, full of mercy and forgiveness, we are most fortunate. Because they are not afraid to identify with the dirt of those they love, marriage becomes a place of healing and hope.

Hatred stirreth up strifes: but love covereth all sins.

—Proverbs 10:12, kjv

# eleven

# THE DELIGHT of FAITHFULNESS

*Love Is Happy with the Truth*
*1 Corinthians 13:6*

THERE ARE MANY FACTORS that need discussion when a man and woman marry—from the challenges of financial security to family stability. These challenges have led to many nuptial negotiations. However, there is one point that is not up for discussion: the truth. A marriage built without the truth is like a structure without a sure foundation. The structure may look attractive, but sooner or later something will come to test the validity and reliability of its foundation.

> These words I speak to you are not incidental additions to your life, homeowner improvements to your standard of living. They are foundational words, words to build a life on. If you work these words into your life, you are like a smart carpenter who built his house on solid rock. Rain poured down, the river flooded, a tornado hit—but nothing moved that house. It was fixed to the rock. But if you just use my words in Bible studies and don't work them into your life, you are like a stupid carpenter who built his house on the sandy beach. When a storm rolled in and the waves came up, it collapsed like a house of cards.
>
> —MATTHEW 7:24–27, THE MESSAGE

Truth has to be the foundation on which your marriage is built. All that is needed is to look in God's Holy Word wherein the truth is written. The Bible deals with every circumstance you will ever face.

Marriages falter because couples have gone away from the Word of God. You can go to church twice a week and not apply God's Truth to your marriage. The real puzzle is, Why go to church without the intent of using God's instructions? That is like going to school and not doing schoolwork.

As a young man, I thought most of what I heard in school was a waste of my time. I rationalized I would not have to use any of that stuff in the "Real World." Upon entering the real world I received a rude awakening. Many of the subjects covered in school were reintroduced in one way or another.

The truth of making your marriage work is discovered in God's Word. The key is not to look in the Bible to improve your marriage, but to focus on improving yourself. Your marriage will improve immensely when you improve you.

## IDENTITY CRISIS LEADS TO IDENTITY THEFT

It has been my observation that far too many marriages suffer when either person is unsure of who they are or what they want out of life. As a generalization, I caution people not to get married before they are 25 years old. I say this only because you should give yourself time to figure out who you are and some of the things you like. It's not impossible to stay married when you're really young (right out of high school) but the odds are stacked against you.

When really young, you are still trying to break away from the hold your parents had on your life. You are attempting to establish some independence. Without possibly knowing it, you are seeking your identity.

People usually receive their identity from cultural backgrounds and social norms. This allows them to be in tune with their ethnicity and their sense of ethics. When you are married it is important to know where your spouse lived as a young person and who raised them. Knowing this will permit you to see what your spouse's beliefs are and what they hold to be true.

When you know where and how your spouse has been nurtured, you have invaluable insight. However, this peaceful state in your marriage becomes impossible to obtain when either partner struggles with who they are.

To struggle with your individual personality is to have an identity crisis. Having this crisis can cause serious trouble in marriage because love finds its greatest happiness in the truth.

There is nothing like being in a relationship where the couple is free to live and love without pretense. I'm talking about not only does your spouse accept who you are but they encourage you to be yourself. When you suffer from an identity crisis (not knowing who you are) you can enter into identity theft (trying to become someone else).

When you become of age you must continue your search of who you are from God's perspective. After all, He created you. Therefore, only He holds the key to whom you must become. Disregarding God's Word and allowing other things to influence your identity places you at risk of becoming someone God has not intended you to be.

People who struggle with their identity try to find solace in becoming someone else. They try to live vicariously through entertainers, athletes or maybe someone a bit closer to home. Instead of taking care of their business, their family, they run off pretending to be something or someone they are not.

This kind of attitude and action places stress on the marriage. Why copy or covet someone else? Rather than trying to be the next whomever, you can work on being the best you. When your spouse married you it was because they loved you not someone else.

Kevin and his wife, Cheryl, were happily married for sixteen years. Then without warning it happened. Kevin would come home and retreat into their bedroom. He stopped talking to the children and would only communicate with his wife when there was a need.

After some time had passed, Cheryl recognized that something was seriously wrong. She convinced Kevin to come in for counseling. After about an hour of trying to assess the problem, our answer became apparent.

Kevin revealed that he was disappointed about his life. Within recent years he had gotten a new house and a job that he enjoyed. However, he said, his friends had (in his estimations) far more than he. Kevin's envy for what his friends possessed had robbed him of the reality of his own success.

Kevin could not appreciate who he was and what he had. Therefore his identity crisis had progressed to identity theft. He secretly wanted to have the life of another. This resulted in the lack of fathering his children and being a husband and friend to his wife.

When you can appreciate who you are and be content with where you are, your marriage will remain strong. We should all desire and strive for growth and development, but stay appreciative of everything we have along the way.

## You Can Handle the Truth

Sometimes getting honesty out of people is like trying to draw blood out of a turnip. The reason people find it difficult to be honest is because so much emphasis is placed on image-management. In other words, we all like to feel accepted by others in some form or way. Therefore, through image management we conduct ourselves according to others' expectations, rather than our own.

Somehow we imagine honesty is not always the best policy. Albeit, honesty is the only policy we should have in marriage. There is nothing you should keep from your spouse. They can handle the truth.

Deliberately withholding vital information from your spouse may indicate you cannot be trusted, i.e. loss of job, excessive spending, internet relationships, etc. In any of these situations you must not withhold information because the effect can be quite damaging.

Base your marriage only on the truth. As long as you are living right and doing what is right in the sight of God, your family will not be hurt. When you live the truth nothing will bring your marriage shame.

Living a life covered with lies means making alliances with the devil. The following scripture amplifies this point:

> You belong to your father the devil, and you want to do what he wants. He was a murderer from the beginning and was against the truth, because there is no truth in him. When he tells a lie, he shows what he is really like, because he is a liar and the father of lies.
>
> —JOHN 8:44, NCV

Let it be understood, truth is the pulse that beats in the very heart of marriage. When your marriage is fortified through walls of truth, trust is established. Your marriage is then free to grow without limits and boundaries.

The devil tries to convince you that your partner cannot

handle the truth. Listen, not only can they handle the truth, I'm willing to bet they demand it. Just live the truth!

I watched an awesome movie starring Tom Cruise and Jack Nicholson, *A Few Good Men*. In this movie, a lawyer (Tom Cruise) is badgering a high-ranking, highly respected military officer (Jack Nicholson). In court, the lawyer is demanding that the officer tell the truth. In a climactic moment, Nicholson's character bellows out to the lawyer, "You can't handle the truth!"

At first glance, one would think the officer is protecting the public from some awful atrocities that plague our society. After careful consideration you discover he was lying to protect himself.

Don't fool yourself! Hiding the truth is for no one's good. The reason why anyone conceals the truth is because of the consequences. My friend, when you stand for what is true; you will have God's protection.

Consider the following commentary on truth:

> The Christian faith is not true because it works; it works because it is true. It is not true because we experience it; we experience it—deeply and gloriously—because it is true. It is not simply 'true for us'; it is true for any who seek in order to find, because truth is true even if nobody believes it, and falsehood is false even if everybody believes it. That is why truth does not yield to opinion, fashion, numbers, office, or sincerity—it is simply true and that is the end of it.[1]
>
> —HANK HANEGRAAFF

The truth calls for responsibility. The minute you are exposed to it you are called to live a life of truth.

Pontius Pilate had the responsibility of deciding whether or not Jesus was to be crucified by the Romans. Upon making his decision, he asked Jesus, "What is truth?" The world has been asking the same question every since.

Listen friend, you can handle the truth because God will enable you. Truthfulness is indicative of faithfulness. Mark it down, the marriage that experiences faithfulness also enjoys fruitfulness.

## FAITHFULNESS BRINGS FORTH FRUITFULNESS

Any marriage not rooted in truth is in trouble. In marriage, when truth is celebrated three things will naturally occur. The truth will build, bond and become bountiful.

The old adage says, "Whatever you put into something is what you get out of it." This has validity, and this principle is found in Scripture.

Matthew 25 depicts a man who went on a far journey and gave his servants various talents. When this man returned, he asked the servants what they had done with their talents. To those who produced and made progress he said, "Well done, thou good and faithful servant: thou hast been *faithful* over a few things, I will make thee ruler over many things" (v. 21, KJV).

It's from this account we establish the principle, "faithfulness brings forth fruitfulness." The master added more rewards to the lives of the faithful servants. And, he refused to add anything to the lives of the unfaithful. Through faith you build, bond and become bountiful in marriage.

## BUILDING YOUR MARRIAGE

> Is there anyone here who, planning to build a new
> house, doesn't first sit down and figure the cost so
> you'll know if you can complete it? If you only get
> the foundation laid and then run out of money,
> you're going to look pretty foolish. Everyone passing
> by will poke fun at you: "He started something he
> couldn't finish."
>
> —LUKE 14:28–30, THE MESSAGE

You definitely need money to build a marriage as well as a
house. However, money alone cannot build it. Money simply
means you have the finances to build your marriage. Again,
building a marriage takes more than having money.

In order to build your house and marriage you need certain
tools. Ask anyone who has been married for a number of years
and they will tell you to erect a marriage takes teamwork.
A positive and constructive effort is needed from both the
husband and wife.

Having this understanding, allows us to see exactly what
tools should be utilized in the building process. If you are
looking for the right tools to build your marriage you do not
have to look further than T.E.A.M. work. I use the acronym
T.E.A.M. for the tools it takes to structure your marriage.

**T**ogetherness: Make plans and work collectively towards
completion. Think "we" not "me."

**E**motional attachment: Share your thoughts about what
helps and hurts your marriage and you.

Affirm each other: Let your spouse know that you're in his or her corner.

Measure your growth: Make sure you are reaching your goals.

## BONDING IN MARRIAGE

As you and your spouse live together you will have opportunities to see each other's vulnerabilities. When this occurs, you must seize the moment to help one another. The acme of any marriage is love. Love always seeks to cover the other's weakness, not expose or exploit them.

I can recall a time when I would complain about Andrea. I saw certain weaknesses in her. However, God asked me two questions.

He asked, "Do you love her?" Then He asked, "Do you feel you are physically stronger than she is?" The answer to both questions was unequivocally, "Yes!" God revealed my responsibility to carry her—because I love her and am physically stronger, He enabled me.

By choosing to carry rather than complain, we declare our love and commitment to succeed.

Bonds are created when people come together and fight for a common cause. This bond occurs whether you are soldiers in war, teammates trying to win a championship or married couples looking to succeed in life. Helping your spouse when they are weak creates a bond. My marriage began to bond when I saw my wife's weaknesses as an opportunity to carry her. And even more when I discovered through my weaknesses, she carried me.

## Bountiful Marriage

The truth gives life. When a couple is truthful with each other this increases the probability of their marriage standing the test of time.

Throughout the years, I have enjoyed watching not just my marriage but many others develop and grow. While counseling couples on the verge of divorce, my advice has been, "Be truthful and watch love flourish." Many of these couples are together today with far more going for their marriage than before.

Every marriage needs time to mature into an environment that is safe and saturated with love. When you are faithful and attentive to your marriage it will grow. Like anything that is nurtured, growth is inevitable. We are safe in truth.

One day, I planted a tree in my yard. Its roots needed nutrients. I placed ropes and stakes around the tree to ensure its proper growth, and I watered it daily. After some time, I did not have to do as much to it as I had in the beginning. The tree continued growing without my constant effort. Now the tree is taller than my house, produces beautiful leaves and provides shade for my family. Your marriage, as you give it nutrients (love) will grow and become fruitful in every way.

Your marriage becomes a haven of rest when you are confident in your identity, operate honestly with your spouse and be faithful. Love is happy with the truth.

# twelve

# TOUGH TIMES DON'T LAST

*Love Patiently Accepts All Things*
*1 Corinthians 13:7*

NORMALLY, IN THE COURTING phase of relationships, marriage is discussed quite blissfully. However, what's ignored are the blisters marriage can create. In the course of every marriage problems will occur. Couples must be steadfast in their love for each other in order to weather the storms of life.

The point of this chapter is that love patiently accepts all things. Some things love accepts can be presented in a negative way, and to patiently accept all things is a tall order. However, all things can be accomplished through love.

## TOUGH TIMES DO COME

When it comes to trouble there are two things that cannot be controlled: *where* trouble hits and *when* trouble hits. There are three main points of trouble that can visit every marriage. Let's consider these areas of tribulation: sex, children and money.

Note: Tribulation can be interpreted as three times the trouble. Jesus encouraged us with these words:

> These things I have spoken unto you, that in me ye might have peace. In the world ye shall have tribulation: but be of good cheer; I have overcome the world.
>
> —JOHN 16:33, KJV

## SEX

Sex is a vital part of the marriage covenant between husband and wife. In fact, marriage is consummated through sex, and should play a part in its continuance.

Wives often complain about their husband's frequent attempts at sex. Wives, I ask you to understand that sex to a man is more than just something physical. The husband's view is, when a wife has sex with him she is expressing her love and appreciation for him. Believe it or not it is emotional to him.

A man views sex like a woman views conversation. It's a form of communication. When a woman rejects the opportunity to have sex with her husband it can be devastating to his ego. Ms, it's like when you want to discuss things with your husband and he says, "I don't want to talk." Imagine not talking to your husband for six months.

Men, we must do a better job at communicating with our wives. This means having conversations about how she feels. Also, we could stand to be more romantic and not rush into sex.

Sex or the lack thereof can cause real problems in a marriage. If there were physical reasons why a spouse could not perform any conjugal act, the other spouse should understand. However, to deny your spouse sex because you never feel like it—that just isn't right. Communicate with one another so unity remains in your marriage.

(Sex and intimacy will be discussed more in Chapter 15.)

## CHILDREN

> Children are a gift from the LORD; babies are a reward.
>
> —PSALM 127:3, NCV

Children are a gift from God. As a gift we must appreciate and take care of our children. Unfortunately, they can present a strain on marriage.

**Scenario 1**

When there's a newborn, the husband can feel neglected. So much of his wife's attention is given to the baby, and arguments can erupt as a result. I speak to these frustrated men by saying, assume some of the child-rearing responsibilities. Start feeding, changing and bathing the baby and your wife will have energy to meet your needs.

**Scenario 2**

Couples can argue about the discipline aspect of child rearing, also. This usually occurs in blended families. A blended family is when one or both spouses bring children from previous relationships into the marriage.

One spouse may doubt the other spouse's love for the child. Therefore, the doubting spouse scrutinizes the disciplining spouse's tactics. This generates problems and could result in fights.

**Scenario 3**

Children can usually detect a strict parent. If given the opportunity, they deal with the parent who gives the least resistance. Children will also play parents against each other. Parents must stand together to avoid division. I am not suggesting that children are malicious. Their intentions are not to cause division; they just want their way.

As adults, it is our responsibility to be mature in all situations. We must ensure our marriage continues to flow in both love and unity.

Finally, we need to know that God is concerned about our children. He will meet their needs better than we can.

Consider the following passage:

> Meanwhile, God heard the boy crying. The angel of
> God called from Heaven to Hagar, "What's wrong,
> Hagar? Don't be afraid. God has heard the boy and
> knows the fix he's in. Up now; go get the boy. Hold
> him tight. I'm going to make of him a great nation."
> Just then God opened her eyes. She looked. She saw
> a well of water....God was on the boy's side as he
> grew up.
>
> —GENESIS 21:17–20, THE MESSAGE

## MONEY

> Lust for money brings trouble and nothing but
> trouble. Going down that path, some lose their
> footing in the faith completely and live to regret it
> bitterly ever after.
>
> —1 TIMOTHY 6:10, THE MESSAGE

Marriage is a bond that should not be broken. Regrettably,
money has caused a wedge in some marriages. It has even sepa-
rated couples.

The adage "money can't buy me love" is true. To some, it can
serve as a great substitute until love shows up. Eventually, all
discover there's no true substitute for love.

> You can't worship two gods at once. Loving one god,
> you'll end up hating the other. Adoration of one
> feeds contempt for the other. You can't worship God
> and Money both.
>
> —MATTHEW 6:24, THE MESSAGE

When you have a heart for God with a desire to please Him, money won't destroy your marriage. Having God's heart allows you to distribute His love. Without God's love in your marriage, money might be the focal point. When money is your only motivation, your marriage will fold under pressure of financial challenges.

> Those who trust in riches will be ruined.
> —PROVERBS 11:28, NCV

If the tribulations of sex, children or money have plagued your marriage, be of good cheer. Jesus has overcome them and He'll help you do the same.

## TOUGH TIMES COME TO TEST

Before we discuss the control we possess over trouble, we need to discover *why* the trouble.

> My brothers and sisters, when you have many kinds of troubles, you should be full of joy, because you know that these troubles *test* your faith, and this will give you patience. Let your patience show itself perfectly in what you do. Then you will be perfect and complete and will have everything you need.
> —JAMES 1:2–4, NCV, EMPHASIS ADDED

I used to own a 1986 Honda Accord. It was old, but it was good enough to get me around.

Every weekday I drove up a steep hill to work. My car would struggle almost to the point of stalling and I despised it. As the car's speed would decrease, my blood pressure increased. Other cars would pass me without effort and I would curse that steep hill.

One morning as my car crawled up that hill, God spoke and said, "The problem is not the hill, it's your car." The hill only revealed that there was trouble under my hood.

In marriage, we experience trouble but trouble reveals areas that need work. Once trouble is revealed, a test is soon to follow. My wife and I have endured many tests, but it was only for the betterment of our marriage.

Consider the patriarch Abraham. He and his wife Sarah had to endure some tough times in their marriage. They had to move away from their family and friends not knowing where they were going. In some cases, they ended up in strange lands and Sarah (due to her husband) ended up in strange beds. Their toughest struggle was patiently waiting years before God would give their promised child.

Their love for each other was proven through these tests. Instead of separating, Abraham and Sarah grew closer. I'm willing to bet the tests tested their closeness. And, because they went through the tests together, God promoted them together.

> And Abram fell on his face: and God talked with him, saying, As for me, behold, my covenant is with thee, and thou shalt be a father of many nations. Neither shall thy name any more be called Abram, but thy name shall be Abraham; for a father of many nations have I made thee.... And God said unto Abraham, As for Sarai thy wife, thou shalt not call her name Sarai, but Sarah shall her name be. And I will bless her, and give thee a son also of her: yea, I will bless her, and she shall be a mother of nations; kings of people shall be of her.
>
> —GENESIS 17:3–5, 15–16, KJV

God called Abraham to ministry and Sarah was to support him. Although Abraham didn't do everything the right way, Sarah stuck by his side.

In contrast, there was another couple who did not fare well in tough times. God called Moses to ministry, and Zipporah was disgusted with him. As Moses set out to do God's will he neglected to circumcise his son. God was seeking to kill Moses, but his wife Zipporah took a knife and circumcised the child (Exod. 4:24).

Zipporah said to Moses, "Surely a bloody husband art thou to me." Needless to say, Moses sent his wife and children back to her father's house. Moses is recorded doing many miracles and mighty works for God. Even still, his wife is not mentioned with him, possibly because of a lack support for her husband. Although he made mistakes, he needed his wife's support.

Sarah was rewarded with promotion along with Abraham. Whenever the name of Abraham is mentioned, the name Sarah is not far behind. In contrast, when Moses is mentioned, you never think of Zipporah. Many people are not aware that Moses had a wife. When Zipporah said you are a bloody husband she was displaying her frustrations. Moses and Zipporah could have been a dynamic duo for God, but this never happened.

Married couples need to understand that the calling of God is not without a price. However, if they stick together they can overcome anything. Trouble comes to test the strength of your marriage and as your marriage goes through the test it is rewarded. As a result of passing the tests, you become better friends and develop a profound respect for one another.

> But God knows the way that I take, and when he has tested me, I will come out like gold.
>
> —JOB 23:10, NCV

Many people may perceive that God causes trouble in their lives. However, God is not bringing trouble to us. He does not arbitrarily cause disaster and destruction in our homes. But, He will use the trouble to His advantage. God is not out to *break us*, His intentions are to *make us* better husbands, wives, parents, people and ultimately witnesses for Him.

> And he shall *sit* as a refiner and purifier of silver: and he shall purify the sons of Levi, and purge them as gold and silver, that they may offer unto the LORD an offering in righteousness.
> —MALACHI 3:3, KJV, EMPHASIS ADDED

The aforementioned scripture relays something vital for our understanding. It pronounces God will sit because He is patient. He knows as we are being tried through fire, we will become better people. Therefore, He sits and He waits.

The same scripture reveals God is a refiner. As the Refiner, God is purging us like gold.

When studying the task of the refiner, I discovered something very profound. The refiner knows the gold is purged and purified when he can see his face in it. Therefore, God is patiently waiting for us to be purified. Creation is waiting for the same.

> We know that everything God made has been waiting until now in pain, like a woman ready to give birth. Not only the world, but we also have been waiting with pain inside us. We have the Spirit as the first part of God's promise. So we are waiting for God to finish making us his own children.
> —ROMANS 8:22–23, NCV

God, like a refiner, is waiting to see His face when He looks at us. God created us to be in His image. Therefore, it's His image that He expects to see. This is why He permits trouble to come our way.

God not only *sits*, He is *silent*. Have you ever wondered why God is silent when you are going through your tests? The teacher never talks while a test is given. And He is the greatest Teacher. He knows we are being developed through our trials. Make no mistake, He is there during the test with you; He's just silent.

The book of Daniel gives us insight to this very fact.

> And these three men, Shadrach, Meshach, and Abednego, fell down bound into the midst of the burning fiery furnace. Then Nebuchadnezzar the king was astonished, and rose up in haste, and spake, and said unto his counsellors, Did not we cast three men bound into the midst of the fire? They answered and said unto the king, True, O king. He answered and said, Lo, I see four men loose, walking in the midst of the fire, and they have no hurt; and the form of the fourth is like the Son of God.
>
> —DANIEL 3:23–25, KJV

The king was able to see Jesus in the fire with the three men. Consider this, the men in the fire never saw Jesus, just the king saw Him. We may not always see God in the midst of our problems, but the devil sees Him.

When tough times come to test our faith and marriage, passing through the fire allows us to pass the test. Having our marriage tested is the inevitable. What becomes important is how we go through the test of tough times.

## TOUGH TIMES COME TO PASS

By now we understand that we have no say in *when* or *where* trouble may strike our marriage. However, we are aware of *why* trouble strikes. Knowing *why* trouble comes gives us control over *how* we handle tough times.

> When the going gets rough, take it on the chin with
> the rest of us, the way Jesus did.
> —2 TIMOTHY 2:3, THE MESSAGE

There's something to be said about tough times and my father says it best, "Tough times don't last, but tough people do." A statement like this lets us know that trouble does not come to stay; trouble comes to pass.

When Hurricane Katrina hit New Orleans, America watched as people's lives were being torn apart. I can vividly recall my heart ached for all those involved.

The hurricane displayed the weakness of the levees; it showed the weakness of our government.

In contrast, the hurricane demonstrated the strength of a nation that was able to unify to provide aid and assistance to those in need. And, the hurricane revealed the strength of people who were able to rise again, though confronted with devastation and despair. Tough times don't last, but tough people do!

Despite tough times, whatever you do, don't fold or give up. Just look up! "If God be for us, who can be against us?" (Rom. 8:31, KJV).

David had some tough times throughout his life. As a young boy he had to fight. Whether it was facing lions, bears, or giants, God was with him. While running for his life, he wrote the well renowned Psalm 23.

Listen to David describe his tough times:

> Yea, though I walk through the valley of the shadow
> of death, I will fear no evil: for thou art with me; thy
> rod and thy staff they comfort me.
>
> —PSALM 23:4, KJV

David called his problem "The valley of the shadow of death."
You may call your problem debt, sickness, unemployment,
infidelity. No matter what you call it, proclaim what David
pronounced. David declared he was walking through the valley
because God was with him. You can declare the same because
God is also with you.

The Scripture declares that God is taking all our trouble and
is using it for our good.

> And we know that all things work together for good
> to them that love God, to them who are the called
> according to his purpose.
>
> —ROMANS 8:28, KJV

The key to your victory, according to the preceding scripture,
is to love God. When you love God right you will love others
right. Friend, love is the key. The devil knows as long as there is
love in your heart for God, there will be love in your heart for
your spouse. The devil desires to separate you from God's love
by bringing as much hell as he can into your homes.

Consider the following text:

> Can anything separate us from the love Christ
> has for us? Can troubles or problems or suffer-
> ings or hunger or nakedness or danger or violent
> death?...But in all these things we are completely

victorious through God who showed his love for us. Yes, I am sure that neither death, nor life, nor angels, nor ruling spirits, nothing now, nothing in the future, no powers, nothing above us, nothing below us, nor anything else in the whole world will ever be able to separate us from the love of God that is in Christ Jesus our Lord.

—ROMANS 8:35, 37–39, NCV

In tough times keep your love for God. Your love for God will manifest through loving your spouse. Love exalts God because God is love (1 John 4:16). When Jesus is lifted up the devil is placed where he belongs—under our feet.

We must be strong in the Lord and in the power of His might. Being strong in the Lord simply means that you trust the Lord will deliver you through any tough situation. It is through trusting Him we are able to sustain any storm.

Make no mistake about it, tough times do come, but they only come to test our faith in God.

With love, learn to patiently wait on the Lord. As God commanded Moses to tell the people, God is commanding us, "Fear ye not, stand still, and see the salvation of the LORD" (Exod. 14:13).

With love your marriage can make it through anything. Never forget, tough times don't last.

# thirteen

# REST EASY

*Love Always Trusts*
*1 Corinthians 13:7*

A S MY WIFE AND I were riding together, we discussed the significance of trust in marriage. She said, "I never really think about trusting you; I just do." Her comment, though pleasing, took me by surprise.

I hate to say it, but before I married Andrea, I was anything but faithful in my dating relationships. However, I always desired to be a trustworthy person, and one day a trustworthy husband. Without ever thinking about it, I had become that man. Andrea's comment in the car was stimulating, but it also served as a warning. I had earned my wife's trust and I wanted to keep it.

Above all, I desire that she can rest easy. And she desires the same for me. Interestingly, our rest depends largely on being able to trust each other.

> A good woman is hard to find, and worth far more than diamonds. Her husband trusts her without reserve, and never has reason to regret it.
> —PROVERBS 31:10–11, THE MESSAGE

I truly trust my wife because her motives are to never do me wrong. She is a good woman and she has the love of God in her heart. I discovered that loving my wife is easy because I trust her.

In God's kind of marriage trust must be extended. Where there is no trust love is in question. I know love is powerful and can be more effective when it is amalgamated with trust.

Notwithstanding, there are a lot of marriages that suffer from a lack of trust. To earn someone's trust certain attributes must be present. Therefore, we need to discuss the effective ways to build trust.

## THE BUILDING BLOCKS OF TRUST

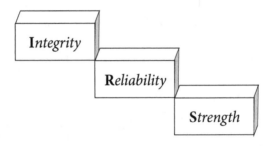

The government of the United States has established an agency called the IRS. This agency collects the taxes of its citizens in order to fund its various needs. Without collecting taxes it would be difficult to pay war expenses, build and repair the infrastructure of cities and pay the services of school teachers, law enforcement, etc. Although taxes may not be favored by citizens, it is required if the U.S. will continue building.

In the same manner, marriage is a building project, a work in progress. However, instead of building through the aid of taxes, a couple should look to build through trust. Taxes are for the welfare of the Nation and trust is for the welfare of marriage.

Because trust doesn't come naturally, it must be built in any relationship. To build trust in your relationship you need the IRS of trust. The IRS of trust comprises three key elements—integrity, reliability, and strength.

*Integrity*—**moral uprightness, honesty, wholeness, soundness**

The first building block of marriage is integrity. Without integrity the other blocks of trust have nothing to build upon.

*Integrity* means to be morally upright and honest. How I conduct business with others determines how my wife views me. If I am disloyal or not honoring my word, my wife will see me as dishonest. If my integrity is in question she will question my loyalty to her.

When you have integrity you are considered a whole person. Your attitude is confirmed with your actions. You don't tell people you have integrity with your lips, you show them with your life.

> Clear my name, GOD; I've kept an honest shop. I've thrown in my lot with you, GOD, and I'm not budging. Examine me, GOD, from head to foot, order your battery of tests. Make sure I'm fit inside and out So I never lose sight of your love, But keep in step with you, never missing a beat. I don't hang out with tricksters, I don't pal around with thugs; I hate that pack of gangsters, I don't deal with double-dealers.
>
> —PSALM 26:1–5, THE MESSAGE

When I was young coming up in the streets of Philadelphia, Pennsylvania, I saw more of my share of dastardly, double-dealing people. I wasn't totally innocent myself. However, when it came to crime, I had my limits and they didn't stretch far.

One day, I was approached by a man coming out of the subway station. While showing me a roll of money, he said he was lost. I thought his actions were rather odd. However, I gave him directions and proceeded on my way.

Moments later, I was approached by another man. This man revealed he had spoken with the first fellow. He made mention of the first guy's money. He suggested he and I pretend to take the first guy where he needed to go and rob him of his cash.

I remember thinking how preposterous and immoral that would be. Conspiring to rob another man went well beyond my limitations. I quickly rejected his offer and removed myself from his presence.

Later, while in contemplation, I realized that both of them were conspiring to rob me. The integrity of my heart kept me from being harmed.

I have seen a lot of people become victims of scams. In many situations, the victim was trying to swindle and was taken by someone better at the game. Those with integrity decide not to play the game altogether.

People who have integrity are elevated in life because they can be trusted. Joseph was a man of integrity.

> And Pharaoh said unto his servants, Can we find such a one as this is, a man in whom the Spirit of God is?...And Pharaoh said unto Joseph, See, I have set thee over all the land of Egypt.
>
> —GENESIS 41:38, 41, KJV

God's Spirit caused Joseph to have integrity. Therefore, wherever Joseph found himself he was trusted. He was trusted above his own brothers, the slaves in Potiphar's house, the prisoners in jail and all the officers in Egypt.

God gave Jeremiah the prophet instructions to search the city of Jerusalem for one honest person. As Jeremiah issued God's polygraph test, he discovered that integrity was in short supply.

> Go up and down the streets of Jerusalem, look around and consider, search through her squares. If you can find but one person who deals honestly and seeks the truth, I will forgive this city. Although they say, "As surely as the LORD lives," still they are swearing falsely. O LORD, do not your eyes look for truth?
>
> —JEREMIAH 5:1–3, NIV

Aspire to be a person of integrity. This will help create a sure foundation in your relationship. When your spouse knows that you have integrity they expect you to be reliable.

### *Reliable*—of sound and consistent character or quality

The second building block of trust is reliability. This means your spouse can depend on you. Helping your spouse through the burdens of life gives them time to rest.

My wife is reliable in many ways. I depend on her for clean laundry, to cook, clean the house, take care of the children, go to work and most importantly, be a faithful and devoted wife. This means so much to me.

Therefore, I strive to be the kind of person she can depend on, too. Andrea can count on me to help take care of our children, cook (especially my pepper steak, *she loves my pepper steak*), pay our bills on time, clean the house (even though our idea of cleaning differs), provide for our family by working and being a faithful and devoted husband. Depending on each other deepens our relationship.

When you are a reliable person your behavior is consistent. You are there when the children experience growing pains, when the financial stability of the home is challenged and when your spouse is going through something. Through every tragedy and triumph—you are there. Being reliable means, you—are—there!

In 1 Samuel 1, the Bible speaks about a woman named Hannah whose husband was there for her. She could not have children and was mocked because of her barrenness. Elkanah (her husband), loved her dearly. He comforted her through her despair and encouraged her in the Lord. Elkanah lived a life of consistency and reliability. Every year without fail, he took his family to the House of God in Shiloh. It was there that his wife received her blessing from God.

A reliable person with sound character exhibits depth and conviction. This person is willing to go the distance and fight for what they believe. If you are not willing to stand for anything, you will fall for everything.

I raised my two sons, Omarr and Vaughn, to be reliable people. Early in their grade school years, I began teaching them to be dependable. I never allowed them to miss school. Omarr graduated from high school without missing one day since the fifth grade. Vaughn only missed two days since the fourth grade and those times were due to surgery.

Were there days they didn't feel like going to school? Plenty of them (especially test days), but they went anyway. No one gave them praise, pats on the back, awards or recognition for this. However, I taught them regardless of accolades to be dependable. Being a person who is reliable means showing up even if the odds aren't in your favor. When your spouse knows that you are reliable they can rest. As a result of resting they are able to trust.

### *Strength*—moral courage; a source of power or influence

The third block used to build trust is strength. Being strong in marriage is displaying moral courage. The term *moral courage* is the ability to make decisions based upon what is right versus *what is right for you.*

One day my family and I were walking into our neighborhood mall. While entering the mall I spotted some money on the ground. No one was around the money so I picked it up and proceeded into the store.

I decided to take the money and buy something for my sons. Suddenly, a woman approached and notified me that the money I had found was hers. I asked the woman to tell me how much she had lost. She gave the exact amount. Therefore, without struggle, I returned what was rightfully hers. Later, my wife said she was proud of me, and that made me glad.

I have witnessed her display moral courage many times. I have watched her return extra change given by cashiers. Many people would argue, "Well, if the cashier can't count they shouldn't be at the cash register." That philosophy might be right for some, but it doesn't make that philosophy right. Moral courage always looks to do what is right.

Giving back what is not yours even when you need it, takes strength and honesty. When your spouse witnesses that kind of strength and moral courage it causes their trust for you to build.

> The Lord spared me because I did what was right. Because I have not done evil, he has rewarded me. I have followed the ways of the LORD; I have not done evil by turning from my God. I remember all his laws and have not broken his rules. I am innocent before him; I have kept myself from doing evil. The LORD rewarded me because I did what was right, because I did *what the LORD said was right.*
>
> —2 SAMUEL 22:21–25, NCV, EMPHASIS ADDED

Sometimes doing the will of God is not easy. However, when you do what is right in the face of tough challenges, God will reward you. Also, your family will see you as honest and honorable thus, giving you their trust.

Consider this: During a class trip to the local pool, a first grade student misplaced her towel. That night, the first grader's mother called the teacher to say someone had stolen her daughter's towel. Trying to calm the mother, the teacher asked her to describe the towel. "It's gray," she snapped, "With Hyatt Regency Hotel written on it!"

Having strength also correlates to having self-discipline. Married couples should always exercise self-discipline. A sure-fire way to accomplish this is through fasting. Fasting is two-fold; it cleanses the body and places it under control of the Spirit. When you deny yourself of impurities you receive the strength of God.

> But Daniel determined that he would not defile himself by eating the king's food or drinking his wine, so he asked the head of the palace staff to exempt him from the royal diet.... The steward agreed to do it and fed them vegetables and water for ten days. At the end of the ten days they looked better and more robust than all the others who had been eating from the royal menu.
> —DANIEL 1:8, 14–15, THE MESSAGE

On many occasions, Andrea has witnessed me fasting and the inner strength I possess. Once, she asked how I was able to fast on only water for more than a few days. I revealed, "My strength comes from the Lord, and I depend on Him to strengthen every area of my life." Having God's Spirit control my life, allows Andrea to trust me. Through trust you learn to rest and go farther than ever imagined.

Other ways to establish trust are:

- Telling the truth
- Spending quality time with each other
- Extending trust

The IRS of marriage can build trust. Subsequently, there is a blockade to trust—jealousy.

## The Blockade of Trust

Having learned about the building *blocks* of trust (IRS), we must not neglect the *block*ade of trust (jealously).

Jealousy is a negative emotion. This emotion occurs when you feel someone is threatening your relationship. Some believe that jealousy proves their love. Although jealousy can display love, it shows fear even more.

You probably have never seen it this way, but it's true. Whenever your thoughts are consumed about what your spouse is doing and who they are doing it with, that's not healthy. You can begin to smother your spouse with unwarranted attention and not allow them the space they need for themselves.

> Jealousy is not a barometer by which the depth
> of love may be read. It merely records the degree
> of insecurity. It is a negative, miserable state of
> feeling, having its origin in a sense of insecurity and
> inferiority.[1]
>
> —MARGARET MEAD

Once you have given into the spirit of jealousy, overcoming that spirit is not easy. Nevertheless, it can be overcome with prayer and if needed, counseling.

My wife is a beautiful woman. As a person, she is great to be around. God created her this way for my benefit and for the benefit of others. It would be wrong of me to keep her hidden like some artifact. I know other men find my wife attractive, and my wife has male friends. Yet, there are boundaries in my wife's male friendships and she doesn't cross them. A friend asked me once, "Do you trust other men with your wife?" I quickly answered, "I trust my wife with other men."

My wife has the love of God in her heart. His Spirit is operating in her life. Therefore, she would never violate our marriage with infidelity. If you allow it, jealousy will block trust, thus, hindering the flow of love. Remember, jealousy is a trap of the devil.

Finally, remain faithful to your spouse. Trustworthiness is absolutely imperative in marriage, and our behavior should always respect the sanctity of it.

Andrea said she never has to think about trusting me; she just does. Well, I would like to say to the love of my life, my feelings are mutual.

*fourteen*

# LOOKING AHEAD

*Love Always Hopes*
*1 Corinthians 13:7*

Praise be to the God and Father of our Lord Jesus Christ. In God's great mercy he has caused us to be born again into a living *hope*, because Jesus Christ rose from the dead. Now we *hope* for the blessings God has for his children.

—1 PETER 1:3–4, NCV, EMPHASIS ADDED

ONE DAY GOD CAME to His creation Adam and announced, "Adam, I'm going to create a woman for you."

Bewildered, Adam asked, "What is a woman?"

With excitement God responded, "Oh, Adam, you're going to love her!"

"Why?" shouted Adam.

God looked Adam in the eyes and began to explain, "Adam, she will cook all of your meals and run your bath water. When you get home from a rough day of work, she'll place you in the bath water and scrub your back."

"Oh, my," Adam interrupted.

God continued, "When your bath is over, she will bring your night clothes and slippers, serve your meal and then sit at your feet for further instructions."

Adam, filled with anticipation, asked, "My God, she'll do all those things? What will it cost me?"

"A rib," God replied.

In shock, Adam asked, "I have to give my rib to get all that? How much can I get for a finger?"

My marriage is fine, but like anything it could stand some improvements. I would love to report that Andrea does for me all God told Adam Eve would do for him. However, like Adam, I'm not willing to give up one of my ribs. Still, that doesn't mean I have to give up hope.

Love always hopes.

When your marriage is not exactly what you desire, don't fret; just keep on hoping.

## KEEP DREAMING

Andrea and I were so excited when we bought our first home. The house was perfect. Every room was just the way we wanted. The backyard was spacious enough for the kids. The front lawn was replete with shrubs and trees.

There was much to like about that house. Yet, there were additions that we desired. After giving it much thought, we created a list of items that would be augmented in the years ahead.

That is how I view marriage. Your marriage can be great; nevertheless, it could always use some improvements. When marrying Andrea, I knew she was the exact woman for me. Notwithstanding, I continue hoping for certain things concerning my wife.

I desire that she experience God in a deeper way. She has an untapped reservoir of knowledge that I hope will one day be revealed. I love my wife and always hope the best for her. Also, she would like to see certain things fulfilled in my life.

Although I am satisfied with my wife, there is much more to see. There's more love, passion, and kindness that she has to offer. Therefore I just keep dreaming. Today, Andrea is a better wife, mother, and friend than she was yesterday. However, I know the best is yet to come.

> People do not hope for something they already have.
> But we are hoping for something we do not have yet,
> and we are waiting for it patiently.
>
> —ROMANS 8:24–25, NCV

Dreaming is so important. Sure, when we moved into our first home we were satisfied. However, we didn't settle. To be satisfied is good, but when you settle you cease from moving forward. Dreaming doesn't allow you to settle. Dreaming takes you from where you are to where you are going.

Jacob was a man with God-inspired dreams (Gen. 28:12), and his ability to dream was inherited by his son, Joseph (Gen. 37:5–9). One day Joseph was kidnapped and taken away from his family; however, he never stopped dreaming. His situation went from bad to better because of his capacity to dream. Not only was he a dreamer, he was capable of interpreting others' dreams (Gen. 40:9–13, 41:15–32).

My point is, no matter what you're facing, whether good or bad, don't stop dreaming. What you hope for today gives you reason to get up tomorrow. If you have stopped dreaming you could be dead and just don't know it.

You never dream for something you already possess. Possessing it would be reality. A dream is something that can't be accomplished without God; it is something hoped for.

Look at Moses, as a child he was raised under the care of Pharaoh's daughter (Exod. 2:7–9). I'm sure his natural mother told him of his Hebrew heritage. I'm certain while Moses grew in the Egyptian palace he witnessed countless mistreatments of his people. And, he must have hoped for the day when he could deliver his people from their burden.

One day, he killed an Egyptian who was beating a Hebrew (Exodus 2:11–12). Moses acted without the help of God, and was forced to flee and hide in obscurity. Several years later, Moses had a God encounter. He received God's instructions and his dream of freeing his people became a reality.

Employ God's help in order to reach your goal in your marriage. God is not only able to help, He desires to help.

## GET YOUR HOPE UP

I have a question. Where is your hope right now? If it's in your friends, family, spouse or government, you have your hope too low. Modern society will warn you not to get your hopes up for fear of a letdown. That philosophy does not correlate with the Word of God. It's time for you and your spouse to get your hope up. When your hope is up, your faith is in God.

> LORD, you are my hope. LORD, I have trusted you since I was young. I have depended on you since I was born; you helped me even on the day of my birth. I will always praise you.
>
> —PSALM 71:5–6, NCV

What do you need in your marriage? Whatever it is both you and your spouse can depend on God. Moses, preparing to introduce God to Israel, asked God for His name.

Read the response that God gave:

> And God said unto Moses, I AM THAT I AM: and
> he said, Thus shalt thou say unto the children of
> Israel, I AM hath sent me unto you.
>
> —EXODUS 3:14, KJV

In essence, God was relating His ability to provide and become whatever we need. There is nothing we can hope for that is out of the reach of God.

> God can do anything, you know—far more than
> you could ever imagine or guess or request in your
> wildest dreams!
>
> —EPHESIANS 3:20, THE MESSAGE

For years my wife and I were trying to have a baby. We did everything we could think of, including what the doctors suggested. I was at the end of my rope and just about out of hope.

Then, one evening while at the conclusion of our annual New Year's Eve service, my father instructed the church to pray for our desires. The thought of a child entered my mind. Yet, I didn't want to ask God, fearing another disappointment.

Reluctantly, I went to God with all humility. It's not that we didn't ask God before, but this night was special. We placed our hope in God and the next year we welcomed my daughter Jada into the world. The very next year we welcomed my daughter Ty. And then we prayed, "God, Sir, please. That's enough." Again, thank You, Lord!

When you place your hope in God, He will move you from the place of not enough, to just enough and finally, more than enough. All God needs is for us, His people, to place our trust in Him.

Facing war, the children of Israel did the only thing they

could do while surrounded by three separate armies. Outnumbered and outflanked, they turned to the One True living God.

> Our God, punish those people. We have no power against this large army that is attacking us. We don't know what to do, so we look to you for help." All the men of Judah stood before the LORD with their babies, wives, and children.
> —2 CHRONICLES 20:12–13, NCV

Whenever your marriage is facing adversity, don't give in or melt down, get your hope up! God sees what you are going through. He is standing ready to deliver you from everything that sets itself against you. Gather your family together and go to God.

Let's look at the results of the war once Israel got God involved. He instructed them:

> You won't need to fight in this battle. Just stand strong in your places, and you will see the LORD save you. Judah and Jerusalem, don't be afraid or discouraged, because the LORD is with you. So go out against those people tomorrow." Jehoshaphat bowed facedown on the ground. All the people of Judah and Jerusalem bowed down before the LORD and worshiped him.... As they began to sing and praise God, the LORD set ambushes for the people of Ammon, Moab, and Edom who had come to attack Judah. And they were defeated.... When Jehoshaphat and his army came to take their valuables, they found many supplies, much clothing, and other valuable things. There was more than

they could carry away; there was so much it took three days to gather it all.

—2 CHRONICLES 20:17–18, 22, 25, NCV

The previous text indicates the Lord fought Israel's enemy. When the fight was through, Israel was able to gather the spoils of war. There were so many valuables it took three days to gather it all. The God who did that for them will do the same for you. Again, He moves you from not enough, to just enough and finally, more than enough. He's not just the God of supply; He's the God of surplus.

All you have to do is get your hope up!

## WATCH WHERE YOU'RE GOING

Brothers and sisters, I know that I have not yet reached that goal, but there is one thing I always do. Forgetting the past and straining toward what is ahead.

—PHILIPPIANS 3:13, NCV

It's paramount in marriage to keep hope alive by looking ahead. When looking ahead, your eyes are on the prize to reach your goals. Albeit, before you can reach any goal, you must set a goal.

A mundane marriage is indicative of a couple that has no goals. My wife and I have set goals that we strive toward finishing. We have individual goals, but more importantly, we have goals we must finish together.

Love is always hoping, always looking ahead. Therefore, as you accomplish things in life, love doesn't stop, it continues moving forward.

It bothers me to hear people say, "I've wasted my life" or

"Had it not been for *this*, I could have accomplished *that*." As long as the flames of love still burn in your heart, you have the opportunity to accomplish whatever you desire. When you love something or someone you do what it takes to experience success.

My grandmother was born into a family of sharecroppers in Greenville County, South Carolina, during the Depression. She walked between seven to eight miles to attend a two-room segregated school, which was not unusual for people who lived in the country.

At age nine, her family moved to Philadelphia, Pennsylvania. She didn't like the city, but as she put it, "I got used to it."

By the time she was seventeen; she was married and had dropped out of school (the eleventh grade). At 21, she had three children. She always planned to go back to school, but things were really rough for a young African-American female with children in the 1940s. Eventually, she had five children and focused on raising her family.

After her mother died in early 1989, she traveled to Copperas Cove, Texas, where she eventually stayed.

At the age of fifty-six, she went back to school. My grandmother completed the requirements and received her General Education Diploma from Central Texas College in Killeen, Texas, when she was 57 years old. She was the oldest member of her graduating class.

The very next year, she passed away and went on with the Lord. Her story is a love story. Before she passed away she had passed her course. Her love for what she desired caused her to look ahead, not back, and accomplish her goal.

Good for you, Grandmom Nellie!

> I have fought the good fight, I have finished the race,
> I have kept the faith. Now, a crown is being held for

> me—a crown for being right with God. The Lord,
> the judge who judges rightly, will give the crown to
> me on that day—not only to me but to all those who
> have waited with love for him to come again.
>
> —2 TIMOTHY 4:7–8, NCV

Love is not frustrated by time. Love patiently waits until the promise or goal is manifested. Like my grandmother, you may have had to postpone a goal or a dream. Don't allow time to dictate the terms. Don't say, "It's too late for me." Look ahead and see yourself fulfilling that God inspired desire. And like my grandmother, you will see your dreams fulfilled.

Paul said, "I have fought the good fight." Although every battle is not worth fighting, there are some "good" fights. What makes a fight "good" is the cause. When it comes to your marriage, there is a cause, so fight the good fight of faith. Don't just see your spouse in their current state, look ahead and see them for who they can become. If your marriage doesn't look good, look again and see it from God's perspective. God sees you as His. You can trust that God takes care of what belongs to Him.

> So we're not giving up. How could we! Even though
> on the outside it often looks like things are falling
> apart on us, on the inside, where God is making new
> life, not a day goes by without his unfolding grace.
> These hard times are small potatoes compared to the
> coming good times, the lavish celebration prepared
> for us. There's far more here than meets the eye. The
> things we see now are here today, gone tomorrow.
> But the things we can't see now will last forever.
>
> —2 CORINTHIANS 4:16–18, THE MESSAGE

My wife and I look at the seasoned couples in our church family and see many quality marriages. I'm not advocating that anyone has a perfect marriage. However, it's good to see couples married over fifty years and enjoying one another.

The Bible says we ought to follow the example of such people. Consider the following text:

> We want each of you to go on with the same hard work all your lives so you will surely get what you hope for. We do not want you to become lazy. Be like those who through faith and patience will receive what God has promised.
>
> —HEBREWS 6:11-12, NCV

Elisha decided to follow after his mentor, Elijah. Elijah asked his successor what he wanted. Elisha said, "I want a double portion of what your life consists of" (2 Kings 2:6-15, author's paraphrase). Elisha decided to look ahead and find someone modeling the kind of life he hoped for himself. He found such a person in his predecessor, Elijah. Elisha was able to live his life serving God and others, as did Elijah.

Marriage takes working together and believing God will bring what He has promised. Like Elisha, Andrea and I decided to look for those with the kind of life and marriage we desire. When looking at the seasoned couples, we see people who have chosen to stay together through good and bad. Through these couples, we see ourselves. In essence, we have learned to look ahead. I know if God can keep them together, He can do the same for our marriage.

Until then, we continue to hope by looking ahead. And one day, Andrea and I will look back and say, "Look what the Lord has done."

*fifteen*

# LOVE LEADS to INTIMACY

*Love Always Remains Strong*
*1 Corinthians 13:7*

*Strong*—having the power of resistance; able to withstand great force or opposition; not easily damaged or overcome.[1]

LOVE IS NOT FORTIFIED through the passing of time. Unfortunately, it is not guaranteed simply by exchanging vows. I have discovered love leads to intimacy, which causes love to remain strong. There is no question love shared in marriage should be strong. However, the question becomes what strengthens love.

Intimacy strengthens love and should be an intrinsic value shared in marriage. It is obtained when you are unafraid to be vulnerable. There are five areas of intimacy that must be shared:

1. Physical—sex (love-shaping)

2. Emotional—how you feel

3. Mental—your intelligence or creativity

4. Social—events or experiences with your spouse

5. Spiritual—your relationship with God

## PHYSICAL INTIMACY

Now, getting down to the questions you asked in your
letter to me. First, Is it a good thing to have sexual
relations? Certainly—but only within a certain
context. It's good for a man to have a wife, and for a
woman to have a husband. Sexual drives are strong,
but marriage is strong enough to contain them and
provide for a balanced and fulfilling sexual life in a
world of sexual disorder. The marriage bed must be
a place of mutuality—the husband seeking to satisfy
his wife, the wife seeking to satisfy her husband.

—1 CORINTHIANS 7:1–3, THE MESSAGE

My wife has an interesting point of view when it comes to sex.
She doesn't like the term "sex" because she feels the term is too
casual. The phrase she has created is "love-shaping."

The most popular idiom for sex is "making love." However,
Andrea believes couples shouldn't be "making love" every time
they engage in intercourse. Her view is once the love between
the couple is established; intercourse thereafter is shaping love.

Love-shaping engages the idea of being in harmony while
developing togetherness in physical intimacy. It gives your
passion purpose—to meet your spouse's needs.

### His needs

A man looks for his wife to fulfill his sexual desires and drive.
Because he should never violate his wife's personal convictions,
it is incumbent upon him to keep his desires and drive within
reason.

In Leviticus 18, God has restrictions concerning a couple's
sex life. According to the Scriptures, everything is not permitted
during intercourse. A major part of love-shaping is discovering

your partner's likes and dislikes. Like God, your spouse may have limitations on sex. Respect their boundaries!

When God commanded men and women to have dominion He wasn't referring to dominance over each other. A display of physical dominance through sexual acts usually indicates a craving for respect in another area of life.

> A right time to make love and another to abstain, A
> right time to embrace and another to part.
> —ECCLESIASTES 3:5, THE MESSAGE

The sexual drive deals with the frequency of sex. I've heard husbands complain, "Sex in my house is like a meal, and I'm starving." There's nothing more frightening than not knowing when your next meal is coming or if it's coming at all. Some men have sex like a holiday—once a year.

I say to the wife who's frustrated with her husband's active sex drive: consider his love for you. His attempts are proof tests of that love.

Remember, men, the sex drive must be kept on manual and not autopilot. A devoted husband's sex drive is maintained under control. If the husband is not controlling his drive, he could succumb to sexual immorality.

And, a good husband desires to please his wife and works to discover her needs.

**Her needs**

A woman wants her husband to facilitate her need for affection and attention.

Affection is met by establishing closeness. Closeness is attained through stimulating conversation. In productive conversation you talk and listen. By listening to your wife she feels validated and valued.

Affection aimed at establishing mutuality in the bed is good affection. As a caveat, if the husband desires his wife to express herself in the bed, he must allow her to express herself outside the bed.

Finally, the husband must give his wife adequate affection and attention. Attention is established when the husband takes notice of her beauty. A wife that is never given attention or told she looks nice can develop low self-esteem.

A story is told of an elderly woman who died. Having never married, she requested no male pallbearers. In her handwritten instructions for her memorial service, she wrote, "They wouldn't take me out while I was alive; I don't want them taking me out when I'm dead."

The wife knows her husband is still interested when he gives her compliments. I give my wife compliments every day. I don't give her compliments so we may engage in love shaping (although, it doesn't hurt my efforts later on). I compliment my wife because she is the apple of my eye and I enjoy letting her know that.

### The beauty of love-shaping

The two personalities of husband and wife make love-shaping beautiful. The love-shaping begins before entering the bed—bare your souls before removing your clothes.

Love-shaping involves eye contact during intercourse. It is not a performance but an expression of two people becoming one. As in dancing, couples flow better when they dance together as opposed to apart.

Originally, dancing expressed emotions, i.e. happiness, anger, etc. Lately, dancing has evolved into physical arduous competition. Many have stopped dancing for fear of not having the right moves or being out of step. In some instances, this has become the case with sex. People feel pressured to perform.

When your sex life has graduated to love-shaping, the only move that is important is the move made to participate.

Note: Love-shaping is more than just having sex.

After having worked all day, Carol came home with an upset stomach and fell terribly ill. She asked her husband Ted to help remove her clothes and assist her to the restroom. Affectionately, Ted began disrobing Carol to help her feel more comfortable.

With his wife disrobed, he began ministering to her needs. Although Carol was nude, Ted's focus was not sex. His concern was helping ameliorate her discomfort. Showing affection and giving attention means we think of our spouse more than ourself.

## Emotional Intimacy

Knowing your spouse emotionally can become a difficult task. People often have trouble expressing their emotions or at least expressing them correctly.

Let's consider John. While dating Michelle, John and she would make frequent trips to the local movie theater. In order to impress her, John displayed no fear when viewing scary movies. And he didn't cry during the romantic ones, either. It wasn't that he didn't experience fear or sadness; he was taught at an early age men shouldn't express these emotions.

Now that they are married, Michelle needs to know how John feels about certain things, yet he is unresponsive. Their marriage suffers because John is not in touch with his emotions.

There are so many emotions that a person can experience. It's important to know what makes us laugh, cry, angry, or sad. And it is important to express these emotions, as well. Knowing how to navigate through your emotional field and your spouse's can be the difference between a happy-fulfilling or hampered-failing marriage.

It is not the responsibility of either spouse to make the other one happy. Happiness is a choice. I often tell my wife, "Choose to have a good day." Your emotions (what you feel) stem from your state of mind (what you think) which reflect your moods (what others see). Therefore, make up your mind to have a good day and your emotions will follow suit.

Today, there is a concept known as emotional intelligence.

> *Emotional intelligence*—consist of the ability to monitor, access, express, and regulate one's own emotions; the capacity to identify, interpret, and understand other's emotions; and the ability to use this information to guide one's thinking and actions.[2]

Be mindful to avoid what causes you or your spouse aggravation and deliver what brings joy. Become familiar with their pains and pleasures.

## MENTAL INTIMACY

"The mind is a terrible thing to waste" is far from an understatement. God created us with the capacity to think and imagine beyond our present state. It is wonderful when couples can challenge one another to do both.

Have you noticed small children always ask questions? My five year old asked me, "Isn't dirt on the ground?" I told her, "Yes." She came back, "If dirt is on the ground, why does your car have dirt on the sides and top of it?" Probing further, she asked, "Did it roll over and play in the dirt?" I just washed my car to avoid explaining the answer. Being around children is good if for no other reason, they cause us to think.

I'll admit at times I might seem like my five year old to my wife. I'm always asking questions. I want to know what she is thinking. I love my wife, and I care about what is on her mind.

I'm the sort of guy who tries to think outside of the box. I tend to prefer the invention over the conventional way of doing things. This is why I write; it causes me to think about how I feel towards many things.

Intellectual stimulation is accomplished through conversation or challenging games. I find most couples that intellectually stimulate each other usually have very good relationships. Whatever method you decide, tap into your spouse mentally. It will keep you both active and creative.

## SOCIAL INTIMACY

All work and no play makes Jack a dull boy (it doesn't do much for your marriage either). There's something to be said for getting outside of your house and spending time with your spouse.

My wife and I aren't social butterflies. We enjoy staying home and catching up on needed rest. Consequently, we look forward to special occasions and being out together. Whether it's catching a dinner and movie or taking a Caribbean cruise; Andrea and I enjoy spending time with each other.

We have aspirations of one day taking a European cruise, visiting such places as Greece, Ephesus, Turkey, Rome, you name it, and we'll go. This year we're planning our visit to Jerusalem. That ought to be a great experience! We take pleasure in visiting our National monuments like Mount Rushmore, the Golden Gate Bridge, Lincoln's Memorial and Niagara Falls.

Spending time together outside our home creates a special bond between Andrea and me. When traveling together, we depend on one another for support and communication. And, a greater intimacy is forged between us because of these different experiences.

Again, you don't have to travel across the country or go globetrotting to build social intimacy. You can go bowling, work out at a gym or stay home and play your Wii. Whatever the event, start doing things together and build memories that will cause your love to remain strong.

## SPIRITUAL INTIMACY

Spiritual intimacy is the most important of all the intimacies. This deals with how you connect with God, and dictates your belief and behavior.

Usually, couples who enjoy spiritual intimacy attend church together. This avoids conflicting doctrines, and lessens the need for counseling.

There are cases when couples do not attend the same church, and are taught the Word of God from different perspectives. This can cause conflict within their marriage. So, if possible, attend the same church. More importantly, develop a genuine relationship with God.

There are also cases where one spouse goes to church and the other does not. In this case, the one who attends church should represent Jesus without condemning the other, and continue praying for the salvation of the non-attending spouse.

Furthermore, couples who experience a relationship with God together are able to raise their children without conflicting beliefs. I know of a couple whose difference in beliefs affects the raising of their children.

When you are connected to God you allow His Word to govern the way you interact with each other. What's more, your marriage grows and prospers.

There's a poem that is read at every wedding we perform in our church. This poem reminds the couple to keep Christ first in their marriage to ensure their spiritual intimacy.

## Marriage Takes Three

I once thought marriage took just two to make a go.
But now I am convinced it takes the Lord also.
And not one marriage fails where Christ is asked to
    enter,
as lovers come together with Jesus at the center.
But marriages seldom thrive and homes are incomplete,
till He is welcomed there to help avoid defeat.
In homes where Christ is first it's obvious to see,
those unions really work, for marriage still takes three.[3]

Through intimacy a bond is fortified that is not easily broken. Therefore, strive for physical, emotional, mental, social and spiritual intimacy in your marriage.

# sixteen

# GAINING POWER THROUGH PRAYER

*Love Never Ends*
*1 Corinthians 13:8, XCV*

A S I BEGIN THE final chapter of this book, I become nostalgic. We began this journey discovering love. And there's no need to find love, if there's no intent to make love last. Through 1 Corinthians 13, we have obtained the picture of love and now finally, we are to ascertain that love never ends.

Ponder that point for a moment; is it really possible to have a love relationship with your spouse that won't ever end? Yes! It is possible, but humor me for a moment.

In *The Wizard of Oz*, there's a young lady named Dorothy. She was lost and desperately trying to find her way back home. In this classical tale, she encounters adventures and new friends. Finally, at the conclusion of her escapade, the Good Witch of the North told her in order to return home she needed to click the heels of her shoes and repeat, "There's no place like home."

Well my friend I'd like to offer this. Of all the different facets you have learned concerning love, keeping your marriage alive does not involve the clicking of your heels, but the submitting of your heart. Instead of repeating there's no place like home, you must focus your attention on the Christian's home. The Christian's home is where the Father lives—Heaven.

> They said they were like visitors and strangers on earth. When people say such things, they show they

> are looking for a country that will be their own.
> If they had been thinking about the country they
> had left, they could have gone back. But they were
> waiting for a better country—a heavenly country. So
> God is not ashamed to be called their God, because
> he has prepared a city for them.
>
> —HEBREWS 11:13–16, NCV

Like Dorothy, we are in a strange land wanting and waiting
to go home to the Father. Until we go home we must keep the
Father's love alive in our hearts as well as in our marriage. In
order to ensure that love in marriage doesn't end, couples must
pray together.

Notice that I didn't say couples must pray, but the emphasis
is placed on praying together.

## COMING TOGETHER BRINGS GOD'S PRESENCE

Have you ever noticed that praying with your spouse can
become a difficult task? It's not that you don't want to pray with
your spouse, it's just that your schedules are so demanding that
you never seem to find the right time.

You need to know the devil's plan is to tire you out through
your rigorous schedules. And, being tired hinders your prayer
life with your spouse.

> And he shall speak great words against the most
> High, and shall wear out the saints of the most
> High, and think to change times and laws.
>
> —DANIEL 7:25, KJV

Praying together as a couple connects your spirits and knits
your hearts. When you pray together, God comes in the midst

of your situation. The Bible teaches us when two or more gather in the name of God His presence is there, and the devil isn't.

Therefore, Satan tries to keep division and strife in marriages to prohibit togetherness in prayer.

The unique quality of praying with your spouse is an intimate matter. The same way you both find the time to steal away from your busy schedules for physical intimacy. you must steal away for prayer. When you pray to the Father, this is a time of closeness, also.

> For Christians, prayer should be its own reward. Prayer is not a magic formula to get things from God. Communicating with God in prayer is itself the prize. Not only is prayer its own reward, but secret prayer is always rewarded by a response from God. While the response we get is not always the response we want, it is the best response.[1]
>
> —HANK HANEGRAAFF

Through prayer you invoke the presence of God into your home, marriage and hearts. Love must stick around your house when God is present because God is love (1 John 4:8).

> Cornelius said, "Four days ago, I was praying in my house at this same time—three o'clock in the afternoon. Suddenly, there was a man standing before me wearing shining clothes. He said, 'Cornelius, God has heard your prayer and has seen that you give to the poor and remembers you.'"
>
> —ACTS 10:30–31, NCV

After this man of God prayed in his home, God was present. The most touching part of this scripture is that God remembered Cornelius. God will remember you and your spouse when you talk to Him.

Prayer not only brings God's presence, it grants God's power.

## PRAYER GRANTS GOD'S POWER

> Confess your faults one to another, and pray one for another, that ye may be healed. The effectual fervent prayer of a righteous man availeth much.
>
> —JAMES 5:16, KJV

The aforementioned scripture states that as couples we should confess our faults one to another. Notice that it does not say we should confess one another's faults. Too often, what hinders our prayer life with our spouse is seeing each other's blunders. However, seeing our own fault is the beginning of seeking His power. God wants to give His power so we can defeat the devil and not live defeated.

A former football player was asked by his coach to do some recruiting. The player agreed then asked, "What kind of player are you looking for?" The coach replied, "Well, you know there's that fellow who gets knocked down and just stays down?" The former player said, "We don't want him, do we?" The coach answered, "No, we don't want him. Then there's that fellow who gets knocked down and gets up and then gets knocked down and stays down." The former player said, "We don't want him either, do we?" The coach responded, "No, and then there's the fellow who gets knocked down, gets back up, gets knocked down, and gets up again and again." The former player said, "That's the guy we want, right?" Then the coach said, "No, we don't want him either. I want you to find me that guy who's knocking everybody down. That's the guy we want!"

As Christians we need to understand the purpose and power of prayer. Prayer is not only for getting back up after being knocked down. It provides the kind of power to seek and destroy the enemy.

The Bible speaks of a man named Samson who was granted power through God. Samson squandered that power through a life of promiscuity. However, while being mocked by his enemies, Samson prayed to God and was granted power once again.

Observe the following account:

> They had him standing between the pillars. Samson said to the young man who was acting as his guide, "Put me where I can touch the pillars that hold up the temple so I can rest against them." The building was packed with men and women, including all the Philistine tyrants. And there were at least three thousand in the stands watching Samson's performance. And Samson cried out to GOD: Master, GOD! Oh, please, look on me again, Oh, please, give strength yet once more. God! With one avenging blow let me be avenged On the Philistines for my two eyes! Then Samson reached out to the two central pillars that held up the building and pushed against them, one with his right arm, the other with his left. Saying, "Let me die with the Philistines," Samson pushed hard with all his might. The building crashed on the tyrants and all the people in it. He killed more people in his death than he had killed in his life.
>
> —JUDGES 16:25–30, THE MESSAGE

The Lord stands ready to hear our prayers, and we need to pray with each other. Please employ the Lord's help through prayer, and God will show you how to be a better husband or wife.

Through prayer His power becomes ours.

## COVER ME, I'M GOING IN

There is power in prayer. As you are praying for your spouse, your intimacy begins to increase and your heart wants to see them do well.

I remember growing up watching those old police shows on television. Whenever the cops would have the criminals cornered in a building, one cop would say to his partner, "Cover me, I'm going in." Well, the same principle applies when it comes to our spouses. They are our partners in life and look for us to cover them in any situation. Unlike cops, we don't use a pistol to cover them, instead we use prayer.

> For the weapons of our warfare are not carnal, but mighty through God to the pulling down of strong holds.
>
> —2 CORINTHIANS 10:4

My wife and I pray for each other every day. As a matter of fact, it's one of the first things I do when I crawl out of bed. I read the Word of God and then I pray for my wife and children. I pray from my heart every day for Andrea and I also have a prayer that I have written concerning her.

Here is a copy of my prayer:

*Heavenly Father,*

*I come to You in the name of Your Son, my Savior, Jesus Christ. I bring before You, Your daughter, my wife, Andrea.*

*Your Word says, "Whoso finds a wife finds a good thing, and obtains favor of the Lord" (Prov. 18:22, author's paraphrase). I thank You, when I found Andrea, she wasn't just a woman, she was a wife. Therefore, she is a good thing for me.*

*Andrea is a virtuous woman and her price is far above rubies. My heart does safely trust in her. Therefore, I pray that she will do me good and not evil all the days of her life.*

*Andrea is a productive woman who works willingly with her mind and hands. Strength and honor are her clothing, and she shall always rejoice.*

*She opens her mouth with wisdom and in her tongue is the law of kindness. May she maintain and display a meek and quiet spirit which is of great price in Your sight, oh God.*

*Since I know that Andrea is a gift from you God, I thank You that she is a prudent woman. She has insight for over sight; she not only makes sound decisions, but she has spiritual discernment in all areas of her life.*

*Grant unto her a courageous spirit and a confidence knowing that she is the beauty found always in my eyes. Outside of You, Jesus, I place her first in my life.*

*I pray to always love my wife as Christ loved the Church. As Christ gave Himself for the Church, I pray to be a husband who will always give of myself for my wife.*

*Father, I ask that Andrea will develop in the Fruit of the Spirit. May she always fear the Lord and have a genuine hunger and thirst for Your Word. I pray that she will meditate in Your Word day and night and will help to teach our children your Word. As she observes to obey it, You will make her way prosperous and give unto her Your good success.*

*May Andrea love, trust and submit to me as her husband. And may she live to commit herself to me as a friend.*

*Finally, I ask that she walk in divine health and live long.*

*I ask these things believing I have received them in Jesus name, Amen!*

As you see, I had to study to make sure that my prayer lined up with the Word of God. Prayers like these create an intimacy that cannot be broken. I invite you to incorporate the previous prayer for your spouse. Just insert their name in the proper place and begin covering your partner today.

Love is the cement in your marriage. Keeping a prayer life is keeping your love alive. Therefore, both you and your spouse should go to the Lord daily and receive His presence and power. As you endeavor to cover one another through prayer, the Lord your God covers you with His love.

# EPILOGUE

WRITING THIS BOOK HAS been a tremendous joy for me. I count myself unworthy of this great task which is to help reconcile and strengthen the marriages that God has ordained.

I began the book *Marriage Matters*, Volume 1, emphasizing that marriage is a covenant two people must honor. I expressed in that book how one need not "fall in love" in order to marry. Marriage is making a choice and living by that choice. However, let me hasten to say, we do need the power of love in marriage. I hope this project, *Marriage Matters* Volume 2, expressed that reality.

How do we experience the power of love in our marriage the way God intended us to?

We must begin by loving God. Jesus is to take preeminence, not just priority in our lives. He is incomparable, incomprehensible and really all that we need. All that we are and ever hope to be we owe it all to Him.

Loving the Lord with the understanding that He loves us unconditionally; allows us to love our spouse properly.

Love is a phenomenon that will take our entire lives to fully appreciate and interpret. It's a wonder of God, a miracle gift, God has graced us to experience. Whatever you do, please don't spend your life pursuing after things that will fade away.

Make it a point, your personal goal, to explore the vastness of love. I pray this book has at least awakened you to love and has caused you to see your spouse in a whole new way. If you are not married, yet, prayerfully this book has deepened your appreciation for love and prepared you to be a loveable person.

Never forget, marriage matters!

May God richly bless you all.

# NOTES

## Chapter 1
### ARE WE THERE YET?

1. Velma Walker and Lynn Brokaw, *Becoming Aware* (Dubuque, IA: Kendall/Hunt Publishing, 2004), 307.

2. John C. Maxwell, *Today Matters* (Nashville: Center Street, 2005).

## Chapter 2
### BE KIND—REWIND

1. *Becoming Aware*, 143.

2. William J. Bennett, *Virtues of Friendship and Loyalty* (Nashville: Thomas Nelson, 2004).

3. Stephen Arterburn, *The God of Second Chances* (Nashville: Thomas Nelson, 2002).

## Chapter 5
### THE SECRET TO MARRIAGE SUCCESS

1. Ronald Youngblood, *Nelson's New Illustrated Bible Dictionary* (Nashville: Thomas Nelson, 1995).

## Chapter 6
### WHERE IS THE LOVE?

1. Andy Stanley, *Like a Rock* (Nashville: Thomas Nelson, 2002).

## Chapter 8
### NOBODY'S PERFECT!

1. Gary Smalley and John Trent, *Love Is a Decision* (Nashville: Thomas Nelson, 2001).

2. *Becoming Aware*, 335.

### Chapter 9
#### That's Three Strikes!

1.      Rick Johnson, *The Man Whisperer* (Ada, MI: Revell, 2008).

2.      Jack W. Hayford, *How to Live Through a Bad Day* (Nashville: Thomas Nelson, 2002),

### Chapter 11
#### The Delight of Faithfulness

1.      Hank Hanegraaff, *The Covering* (Nashville: Thomas Nelson, 2009).

### Chapter 13
#### Rest Easy

1.      *Becoming Aware,* 304.

### Chapter 15
#### Love Leads to Intimacy

1.      *Reader's Digest Oxford Complete Wordfinder* (Chappaqua, NY: Reader's Digest Association, 1999).

2.      *Becoming Aware,* 191.

3.      "Marriage Takes Three" (n.p.: All Good Books, 1983).

### Chapter 16
#### Gaining Power Through Prayer

1.      Hank Hanegraaff, *The Prayer of Jesus* (Nashville: Thomas Nelson, 2005).

# ABOUT THE AUTHOR

TYRONE HOLCOMB RECEIVED CHRIST in 1986. He has experienced God's mercy, grace, and love in his own life firsthand, thus making his teachings relevant, encouraging, comforting, refreshing, and always on the cutting edge. His understanding of the good news of Jesus Christ coupled with the revelation that it's all about Him makes him a vessel that God can use in this hour. He is proudly on staff with his father, Bishop Nate Holcomb, in Central Texas. He is a part of the preaching/teaching ministry team. Tyrone Holcomb's wife, Andrea, and their children, Omar, Vaughn, Jada, and Ty, are very much a part of the ministry.

# TO CONTACT THE AUTHOR

tholcomb@chop.org